WOMEN OF HOPE

by Jennifer Mathewson Speer

Hope in the Lord!
Jennifer Mathewson Speer
Hebrews 6:19

OUTCOME
PUBLISHING

Women of Hope

Published by Outcome Publishing
1510 1st Avenue West #102
Bradenton, Florida 34205
www.outcomepublishing.com

Unless otherwise indicated, Bible quotations are taken from The Holy Bible, New American Standard Version. Copyright © 1960, 1962, 1963, 1968, 1971, 1972, 1973, 1975 by The Lockman Foundation.

First Edition

Printed in the United States of America

1. Religion: Spiritual General
2. Self-Help: Spiritual
3. Religion: Christian Life – Personal Growth

In memory of my father
__Haywood Cosby__
Wonderful!

Out of the ashes...hope is born.
Dedicated to my grandchildren
Cooper
Callie
Piper
Judah
Maxine

CONTENTS

FORWARD

Lettie Kirkpatrick Whisman

It is a scary thing to face life without hope – scary
enough to make us despair of living. I know . . . I camped there
for a season of life that I now refer to as my refiner's fire. One
of the lessons I gleaned from that fire is that even when I could
not hold onto God, He never let go of me.

Ironically, my writing and speaking ministry were
built to extend hope and encouragement to the audience God
placed in my path. My three word mission was "holding forth
hope". My scripture declaration was "I have put my hope in
your word." (Psalm 119:114) I guess it is also no surprise
that the enemy of my soul would attack at that very place of
confidence.

Jennifer and I are no strangers to watching each other
fight for hope. She will write with transparency and readers
will be blessed to know of her own battles in the powerful
and truth saturated pages of this book. In the years of our
friendship, I have witnessed first hand her journey on the roller
coaster of trying to "feel" hopeful. And she has seen mine.

Jennifer "happened" to show up at the hospital during
my husband Phil's ICU days as I did vigil at the beginning of

the massive stroke that changed our lives, destroying the world as we knew it forever. I was stunned and disbelieving at the turn of events that came during what seemed a season of restoration.

Phil and I had married following the deaths of our spouses from cancer. In a few short, happy years together, we rejoiced that God seemed to have brought us into a new time of joy. The promises we had clung to in dark days were true after all! Our hope in God's goodness and redeeming were well placed. Really?

That day, with Phil in ICU, now a functioning mind trapped in a useless body, Jennifer heard my agonizing questions about this God who gave us hope for happiness, then allowed this total destruction of our lives.

Yes, hope took a hit during my refiner's fire. But God's anchor held for me when I couldn't imagine it was even there. That is because Jesus was my hope and truth trumps feelings, even the feeling that hope is lost. And the truth is, He never leaves or forsakes us.

I read Jennifer's first book, *Women of Grace*, from my place on the couch, after I put Phil down for the night in his hospital bed in our kitchen. My tears often flowed as I was reminded of God's power and the redemption that comes through His overwhelming grace.

I will read *Women of Hope* from another season – knowing the reality that Jesus is my hope and in Him I am anchored and secure . . . no matter the season. I commend to you *Women of Hope*, confident you will be blessed, encouraged, and rejoicing as this work of God through His servant adds insight and foundation to the reality that, in Jesus, our soul's anchor will truly hold.

Lettie is a popular author and speaker residing in East Tennessee. Her writing has appeared in over forty publications and she is also the author of four books. Her most recent book is *God's Extravagant Grace for Extraordinary Grief.* For information about Lettie's ministry, visit www.WritingForHim.com

INTRODUCTION

Several years ago I unexpectedly received a Christmas card and letter from a longtime friend. Over the years life had unfolded, taking us in separate directions. Consequently, we hadn't talked in ages. I was thankful the letter and card was later followed up with a phone call.

As we quickly caught up on family and careers, we also shared life's disappointments, tragedies, and struggles—realizing we both seemed to have had more than our fair share. In the midst of our conversation, the subject of hope came up and the question was raised, "Is there really hope for everyone?" I pondered the answer for days. In fact, the Lord used that timely conversation and question as the catalyst for this book.

Several weeks later, I heard a Christian radio host say, "Every person needs to know three things: to know they are loved, to know life has purpose, and to know there is hope" (Carmen, *The Joy FM*). There it was again. That word. *Hope.* Yes, everyone needs it, but can everyone experience it? My pondering drove me to Scripture, thirsting to understand God's perspective and His answers to my growing questions about hope.

Perhaps my initial quest for truth was for the sake of my longtime friend. The Lord, however, expanded my quest to include the women I teach in Venice, Florida. For eight weeks, several hundred women patiently waded with me through studies and questions about hope. Their encouraging response to our study led me to write my second book, *Women of Hope*.

Hope is one of those words we use a lot in religious circles but rarely define. Unfortunately, the English language almost exclusively defines *hope* as *"wishful thinking."* Even in writing this book, I had to constantly remind myself that wishful thinking is far from Biblical hope. Certainly as Christians we agree Christ is our hope, but what does that mean in the day to day of life? How can we experience hope every day? And why do we sometimes feel hopeless?

Seven women in Scripture give clear answers to questions about hope. With the exception of one, each woman experiences a crisis of hope. Some of these women lose sight of hope, and others will hear for the first time hope is real and waiting just for her. I have learned to love these women because, like you and me, they need hope. They need an anchor in the turbulent circumstances of life. They need joy, peace, and purpose in a world that offers nothing but brokenness. Like us, they need *"...the God of all hope..."* (Romans 15:13).

I pray you will be encouraged as you read. Hope is indeed for you, dear one, no matter what you have suffered or experienced—no matter what you have done or what has been done to you. Hope is real because hope is in Christ. He is the anchor for your soul.

1

HOPE
An Anchor for the Soul

Since moving to Florida, my husband's work in the aviation industry provides the privilege of associating with pilots on a daily basis. Through his work, however, we have learned aircraft pilots have a reputation for being adventurous. No matter how safe they might be in the air, many pilots are thrill seekers in other areas of life. Two of our friends, Luke and Greg are young pilots who fit this description perfectly. They each have a thirst for adventure which includes scuba diving.

One morning, Luke and Greg set out into the Gulf of Mexico despite weather warnings of a coming storm. They were determined to have a day of scuba diving, believing they would return to shore before the storm hit. The two pilots took Greg's small boat several miles out into the Gulf. They anchored the boat and threw out the diving buoy, marking their location as well as warning other boaters of scuba divers beneath. It began as a glorious day for diving.

An hour into the dive, the pilots could see the sunlight above them fading. The water grew darker and flashes of lightning could be seen from their position underneath. Motioning to each other that it was time to head for the boat, they surfaced. To their dismay, the storm was upon them. Dismay quickly turned to terror when they realized the boat was gone. *The anchor did not hold*. The boat was lost in the storm. The pilots, wearing heavy scuba gear and no life jackets, were aimlessly bobbing in a tumultuous ocean. They were stranded with little hope of ever being seen or rescued.

Luke later recalled his relief when a small fishing boat racing back to port miraculously spotted their diving buoy and turned to investigate. The two pilots were rescued. The missing boat was later found far from the diving spot, dragging its unattached anchor. Certainly the misery of that diving day could have been avoided if our friends had not encountered a storm. But the terror of that day would have been averted if only the anchor had held.

Hebrews 6:19 says, *"This hope we have as an anchor for the soul, a hope both sure and steadfast...."* Unlike the anchor of our pilot friends, the hope we have as believers in Christ is steadfast and sure. It does not let go. It anchors our souls. Yet as a teacher, my mind wants to know the answers to questions about hope. What is Biblical hope? What is it not? How do I get this hope? Can I lose hope? How does it anchor my soul? And what is a soul anyway?

The Greek New Testament word for hope is *elpis*. As a noun in secular Greek as well as in English, it means *the desire for something good*. However, the Biblical definition has a fuller meaning. It is *the desire for something good and the confident expectation of receiving it based on the Word of God and the character of God*. Hope is forward looking, filled with anticipation that God will keep His promises, doing all He says He will do. Hope is about the future, but the future does not simply mean our eternal home in Heaven. Hope applies to everyday living as well.

Paul prays in Ephesians 1:18 that the eyes of our heart would be enlightened so we can know the *hope of our calling*. Paul is certainly including Heaven as part of *the hope of our calling*, but Heaven is not our entire hope. The *calling* in Ephesians 1:18 is our call to salvation. When God called us into a relationship with Him, He then blessed us with everything we need to live victoriously in that relationship. In fact, Ephesians 1 reads like a laundry list of what is ours in Christ. In the original language, Ephesians 1:3-14 is one sentence. It is the longest sentence in the New Testament. The words *in Him* or *in the Beloved* or *in Christ* are attached to every blessing listed in this long sentence.

Paraphrasing Paul, when we become Christians, we get all of Jesus we are ever going to get. We do not get Jesus in increments. We do, however, spend our entire lives learning to live in all we have been given at salvation. Philippians 1:6 states, "*I am confident of this very thing, that He who began a good work [the call to salvation] in you, will complete it [perfect it, mature it] until the day of Christ Jesus.*" The completing, perfecting, or maturing of believers is the lifelong process of sanctification.

So as we begin our study about *hope in the everyday circumstances of life*, we must keep in mind **Christ is the centerpiece of our hope**. God initiated a relationship with us, and He will complete the good work of salvation—because of Christ. Furthermore, as believers, God has made everything available to us for abundant and victorious living—because of Christ. Finally, believers have the privilege of living in the confident assurance (the hope) that whatever God has promised, God will do---because of Christ. Joyfully, we can agree with Paul, "*Christ Jesus, who is our hope*" *(1 Timothy 1:1).*

So how does hope anchor my soul? And what is a soul anyway?

It is interesting to hear ship captains and airline captains refer to those on board the vessel, not as people, passengers, or customers—but as *souls*. There is depth to the word *soul*. The Bible uses the word 459 times. It is first used in Genesis 2:7, *"And the Lord God formed man of the dust of the ground, and breathed into his nostrils the breath of life; and man became a living soul" (KJV).* The New Testament word for soul is *psuche*. It simply means *"to breathe"*. Dear one, you do not simply *have* a soul—you *are* a soul.

In his book *Soul Keeping*, John Ortberg quotes his mentor and friend, the late Dallas Willard. Dr. Willard asserts, "You are a soul made by God, made for God, and made to need God, which means you were not made to be self-sufficient" (John Ortberg, *Soul Keeping* p.39).

John Ortberg further explains Dr. Willard's teaching about the soul. "Your soul is what integrates your will (your intentions), your mind (your thoughts and feelings, your values and conscience), and your body (your face, body language, and actions) into a single life. A soul is healthy—well ordered—when there is harmony between these three entities and God's intent for all creation. When you are connected with God and other people in life, you have a healthy soul" (*Soul Keeping*, p.43).

Interestingly, when our soul is anchored—when it is healthy— our circumstances do not dictate the wellbeing of our soul. The story behind the famous hymn *"It is Well with My Soul"* is a moving example of a soul anchored in Christ in the midst of bad circumstances.

Horatio Spafford was a successful lawyer and businessman living in Chicago during the 19th century. Although he was a devout Christian, difficult circumstances punctuated his entire adult life. His young son died and soon thereafter, Spafford lost his entire fortune in the Chicago fire of 1871.

In 1873, he planned a European vacation for his family but business developments prevented him from traveling with his wife and four daughters. Spafford placed his family on the S.S Ville du Havre in November, 1873. He expected to join them in England a few days later. Unfortunately, the Ville du Havre was struck by another sea vessel and sank in 12 minutes. Mrs. Spafford was rescued but all four daughters died. Once in England, Anna Spafford sent a telegram to her husband, "Saved alone."

Horatio Spafford boarded another vessel to meet his wife. He asked the captain to inform him when the ship was approaching the area where his daughters had drowned. The captain did so and at that fateful spot, Horatio Spafford penned the words to the now famous hymn (Michael Haun, The History of Hymns).

**When peace like a river, attendeth my way,
When sorrows like sea billows roll;
Whatever my lot, Thou hast taught me to say,
It is well, it is well with my soul.**

Recently, I was sent a captivating photograph which brought me to tears. A family friend, who was also a pastor, died after a lengthy battle with pancreatic cancer. The photograph was taken at his funeral service. In the picture, family members were singing a medley of songs, which included "It is Well with my Soul." Tears came to my eyes when I saw in the foreground of the photo a single hand raised high in praise to the Lord. It was the hand of the pastor's widow, she too dying of cancer.

The photograph of my friend's funeral captured the sadness of loss but also the brilliance of the hope. A hope that is able to testify to the goodness of the Lord even in difficult circumstances. A hope that provides a sure and steadfast anchor in both living days and dying days. A hope that does not exempt us from difficulties but indeed grips us in the midst of them. Christ is our hope. He is the anchor that holds—every single time.

"Why are you in despair, O my soul? And why have you become disturbed within me? Hope in God, for I shall again praise Him for the help of His presence (Psalm 42:5).

Boundaries and Responsibilities

Defining hope as "desiring a good thing and having the confident expectation we will receive it based on the Word of God and the character of God" includes boundaries as well as responsibilities. We need to understand *what hope is not* in order to gain a solid understanding of Biblical hope. We must explore the boundaries or perimeters of hope.

Hope is **not** wishful thinking. The English language often uses the word *hope* to convey a wishful sentiment. "I hope we can go." "I hope you can stay." "I hope I make more money." We could easily insert the word *wish* instead of the word *hope*. However, Biblical hope is not wishful thinking. Neither is it positive thinking. It is not coming up with a plan, crossing our fingers, and wishing (or even praying) hard enough for God to finally relent and fulfill it. Hope is not our perception of how things should be or how we want them to be. Neither is hope based on feelings. Emotions will tell us we are hopeful when the feeling of hope is present and hopeless when the feeling is absent. But we cannot live victoriously if we are constantly waiting for the emotion or feeling of hope. Sometimes it just isn't there—and yet, in the absence of positive feelings...Hope remains.

Hope is based on truth. Truth is the unchanging, unfailing Word of God that flows from the steadfast character of God. Hope abounds because of all we are and all we have in Christ simply because God says so! He does not change and He cannot lie. This is why hope anchors us. Our hope, Christ, is unfailing and unchangeable. He does not wax and wane according to circumstances or feelings. He is steadfast and sure. Therefore, so is hope. Hope remains even if the believer does not feel it, even if the believer cannot see it, and even if the believer temporarily does not believe it. Hope is not based on us. It is based on Christ. The anchor holds, hope holds, because our hope is Christ.

As Christians, however, we have the privilege and the choice of living each day in hope—or not. We have the daily responsibility to cooperate with God, to surrender to His ways, His plan, and His truth. How do we do that? How do we live in the hope that is already ours?

Live with a renewed mind. There are countless passages of Scripture that refer to our minds. There are, however, a few basic truths we would do well to explore.

Paul admonishes Christians to "*...be renewed in the spirit of your mind*" (Ephesians 4:23). He also tells us to be "*...transformed by the renewing of your minds*" (Romans 12:2). Neither of these statements just magically happens when we come to know Christ. Henry Blackaby reminds us the renewing and transforming of our minds is a daily process that occurs as "the Spirit of God uses the Word of God to teach us the ways of God" (Henry Blackaby, *Experiencing God)*

We cooperate with God as we daily read, study, meditate, memorize, and in any way, digest the Word of God. Cooperating with God requires us to open our Bibles and set our eyes and hearts on the Word. The Spirit of God uses the Word of God to change the way we think. As our thinking is changed, our behavior is changed as well. Warren Wiersbe says, "What you believe determines how you behave."

This process of renewing the mind **IS NOT** behavior modification. The Word of God is active and alive, a two-edged sword that convicts and confronts, disciplines and matures, teaches and encourages (Hebrews 4:12). The Spirit uses The Word to change us from the inside out, **not** the outside in (Ephesians 3:16).

Our thinking, not our circumstances, must change if we are to live in hope. We live in a society that often values feelings above truth. Feelings are not invalid, but neither are they the rudder that guides the ship. Truth must guide us. The Spirit and The Word train our minds to always anchor in truth. Feelings may or may not follow, but certainly they cannot lead. In fact, wrong thinking will always lead to wrong feeling. Therefore, Paul emphatically states three times in Ephesians 6, "*stand firm.*" It means "hold your position at a critical time in battle". *Do not give up ground already won.* Our hope has already been won. We must stand firm in truth. Truth is the Word of God, transforming and renewing our minds.

Two final passages about truth and the way we think are worthy of noting. Psalm 119 is the longest chapter in all of Scripture—176 verses. Every verse points us to the value of God's Word in our lives. Additionally, the Apostle Paul writes, "*Finally brethren, whatever is true, whatever is honorable, whatever is pure, whatever is lovely, whatever is of good repute, if there is any excellence and if anything worthy of praise, let your **MIND** dwell* [settle down and live there] *on these things*"(Philippians 4:8). We learn what is true, honorable, pure, of good repute, excellent, and praiseworthy as we digest the Word of God.

Please note! I am not saying if we read the Bible enough we will be healed of all the ailments of body, mind, and soul. Knowing, believing, and resting in Truth did not raise my dead husband's battered body; it has not cured all my diseases; it does not guarantee a life free of struggle. Truth, however, is the light that shines at our feet on the darkest night—

illuminating the next step (Psalm 119:105). As our minds are renewed and transformed by truth, truth becomes the light that guides our decisions, our choices, and our reactions. Truth is the place to stand, even if we cannot feel or see or understand our hope. Personally, I have wrestled with God on many issues: death, grief, sin, cancer, depression, and prodigals. Eventually, I must always come back to rest in His Truth. There may not always be happy thoughts and serene circumstances, but in spite of it all, Truth anchors my mind in the hope I have in Christ. Dear believer, He will not let us go. He will finish the good work of sanctification which He began.

Live by faith. It is great to have our minds renewed, but at some point we have to just get up and live it. This is where faith comes in. Faith and hope are closely aligned in Scripture. 1 Corinthians 13 and Hebrews 11 are passages that put the two concepts together. Hebrews 11:1 says, *"Faith is the assurance of things hoped for. ..."* We would do well to define faith before we try to connect it with hope.

Missionary and author Avery Willis defines faith as *"acting on revealed truth" (MasterLife)*. I like that definition. It fits well with a careful study of Hebrews 11. Sometimes we have assigned faith to only a few super Christians, those who dare to do big and bold things for God. Yet all of us have been invited to live by faith. In fact, we have been commanded to live by faith.

Faith, however, does not simply mean believing harder. James 2:19 tells us even the demons believe. Neither is faith claiming something in Jesus name and then expecting God to come through. That is presumption! Faith is acting on the truth God has already revealed. Hebrews 11 gives us many examples of faith. Each person listed in Hebrews 11 is told something by the Lord. The person believes it and then trusts God enough to do it—to act on it. That is faith. Faith is really not complicated. It is not a leap into the dark. It is an obedient step into the light of truth. Rarely does God illuminate the entire path through the forest. He does, however, give us enough truth, enough light, to take the next step. When we take it, we are walking by faith.

Let me give a personal example.

December 2013, I was diagnosed with cancer. I was scared to death. But no matter how much I prayed and how often I searched the Scripture, I never found a promise saying God would, on a certain day and time, completely, physically heal me. In fact, I had no assurances in this life I would ever be healed. Now I had a choice—would fear be my focus or would Christ be my focus?

Philippians 4:6 tells me, *"Be anxious for nothing BUT in everything by prayer and supplication with thanksgiving, let your requests be made known to God. And the peace of God which surpasses all comprehension will guard your hearts [feelings] and minds [thinking] in Christ Jesus."* Certainly I believed this truth, but I had to also act on it. I had to stop wringing my hands and start praying, laying my fears and worries as well as my desires before the Lord. Then I had to thank Him in advance for whatever answer He chose to give. Doing these seemingly simple things was an act of faith. And God kept His word. He guarded my mind and my heart with peace—with NO promise of physical healing.

Three years later I am cancer free, **but I am NOT cancer free because I had great faith!** I am well because that is simply how God chose to work at this time. Faith is not claiming something big in Jesus name and assuming God will come through. Faith is walking in the truth we have been given in His Word, trusting Him even when we cannot see the end result. I still have no guarantees about cancer returning. However, I have full assurance that He is standing guard over my soul, ready to give peace—even if cancer returns. For all of us, trusting God enough to obey Him is living by faith.

Hope is a part of faith. Everything we are and everything we have been given in Christ is our hope. Now we act on it. That is faith.

Here are some examples of hope and faith working together:

Our hope (confident assurance) is forgiveness of sin (1John 1:9). **Now in faith**, we confess and repent and receive the forgiveness we are offered.

Our hope is God will finish the good work He has started in us (Philippians 1:6). **Now in faith**, we learn, trust, and obey His Word while He completes the work.

Our hope is we have the mind of Christ (1 Corinthians2:16). **Now by faith**, we allow the Spirt of God to use the Word of God to transform and renew our minds.

Faith and hope are linked. We have hope and we learn to live in it by faith. To walk fully in the hope that is already ours, our faith must grow. Faith grows in two ways. First, faith increases by the Word of God. *"Faith comes by hearing, and hearing by the Word of Christ"* (Romans 10: 17). The more we know His Word, the more we trust Him. The more we trust Him, the more we obey Him.

The second way God grows our faith is through trials and difficult circumstances. James 1:2-4 says we are to count it all joy when we unexpectedly fall into various degrees of trails. In the trials, God produces endurance in us. Endurance, in the Greek, means *the ability to remain under*. God is not often interested in rescuing us out from under our trials. Instead, He allows us to remain in the trial so that in His strength, we gain endurance. Endurance then perfects and matures our faith.

If Christians are to live daily in hope, they must live daily by faith as well. God's desire is to increase our faith through His Word and through our circumstances.

Live in the Spirit. Among Christians, there are various interpretations and teachings regarding the Holy Spirit. While certainly some teachings about the Holy Spirit are divisive, we cannot ignore the power and energy of a victorious Christian life. The Holy Spirit of Christ dwelling in us is the source of power. He is the power who uses the Word to transform our minds. He is also the power who enables us to live by faith. He even gives us the desire to live by faith (Philippians 2:13). If we desire to live in hope, we must live in the power of the Holy Spirit and under His control.

Ephesians 3:16-17 are key verses in understanding the role of the Holy Spirit in our lives as it pertains to hope. "*... that He (God) would grant you according to (in proportion to) the riches of His glory, to be strengthened with power through His Spirit in the inner man: so that Christ may dwell in your hearts through faith. ...*"

God goes to work on the inside of us. He uses the Holy Spirit to strengthen us in the inner man. The inner man includes our mind, our emotions, and our will. The Spirit wants Christ to dwell in our hearts (our inner man). *To dwell* means to settle down and live. It is God's desire for His Spirit to permeate every aspect of our inner being. He wants access into the secret places, the hidden thoughts, the off- limit habits, and the never-seen-or-heard thought processes. He wants to clean it all out and replace it with Christ. Then Christ can be at home in every nook and cranny of our lives. When Christ permeates our inner man, we begin to see and understand the hope that is ours. We desire to live obediently in that hope. When the inner man begins to change, the outer man reflects those changes in word and deed. The Spirit is the energy for the transformation taking place.

Finally, Romans 15:13 sheds more light on both the Spirit and hope. "*Now may the God of hope fill you with all joy and peace, as you trust Him that you may abound in hope by the power of the Holy Spirit.*"

God is not the dispenser of hope. He **is** hope. As we trust Him and yield to Him, He fills us with joy and peace until we overflow with hope. This filling to the point of overflowing is a continuous, daily work of the Holy Spirit in the inner man.

In closing, every believer has hope because every believer has Christ. Only one question remains, "Can we lose hope?" The resounding answer is "NO!" Ephesians 1:13-14 says we are sealed with the Holy Spirit of promise. To be *sealed* means our relationship with Christ is permanent and authentic. The transaction is complete, never to be undone. The Spirit is also a pledge, a down payment of all that is yet to be----both here and hereafter. Our hope does not come and go because Christ in us does not come and go. He is faithful even when we are not. His residency in our life is based on His character and His Word, not our works, performance, or circumstances.

We can, however, lose sight of hope. We can also lose the feeling of hope. Many things contribute to these losses. Sickness of mind and body can make us feel hopeless. Difficult circumstances can cloud hope. Sin can cut us off from the feeling of hope. Yet for each dilemma there is an answer. Medical attention, counselors, praying friends, and a community of accountability are all instruments God uses to redirect us back to truth and then help us apply truth to our lives.

We lose sight of hope when our soul is unhealthy, when we are out of sync with the Lord and other people. When any cylinder of a car engine stops working or becomes damaged, the car doesn't run effectively. People are similar. If we want to live victoriously as believers in Christ, every facet of our souls must be finely tuned. Therefore, it matters what we put into our bodies. It matters what we feed our minds. It matters who we associate with. It matters what we believe, and it matters how we behave. Otherwise, our soul becomes disjointed and unhealthy, and we easily lose sight of hope.

When my late husband and I first moved to Knoxville, Tennessee, we were thrilled by the beauty of the Smoky Mountains. Every day, I would drive to church or school, heading across a plateau and then taking a left turn down into the valley. The view of the mountains as I drove into the valley was spectacular. Ridge after ridge of majestic mountains unfolded in front of me. I gasped every time I took in the scene.

We lived in Knoxville for thirteen years, and I soon discovered my perception of the mountains could easily be altered. In the spring and fall when temperatures changed, a fog would settle into the valley and obstruct my view. In the hot summertime, a haze developed and prevented a clear look at the mountains. In the winter, low, gray snow clouds often hung around for days, creating a dreary climate as well as blocking out my treasured view. But I lived in those Smoky Mountains long enough to realize, in spite of the weather or my vantage point, the mountains remained. They were steadfast and unmovable even in the fog, the haze, and the clouds. My view may have been altered, but the mountains were not.

Biblical hope is similar to the mountains. Sickness, circumstances, and sin can certainly change our perception, but none of these things can change our hope.

The next seven chapters will explore the lives of women in Scripture who either have been given hope or are in a crisis of hope or need hope. They are women like us. Women who face difficult circumstances, juggle responsibilities, and often need to be reminded of their hope in Christ. Their souls need to be anchored—just like ours. As you read, rest in the truth: Christ will not let you go. No matter where you have come from or where you are going, He is the faithful, unmovable, unchangeable anchor for your soul.

Discussion Questions

1. How is Biblical hope different from wishful thinking? What comfort does that bring you?

2. After reading the story of Horatio Spafford, are you surprised he could write the hymn *"It Is Well with My Soul"*? How can our soul be all right when everything in our world is all wrong?

3. Hope remains even when we lose sight of hope because hope is based on the faithfulness of Christ. What are some things that cause us to lose sight of hope? Has there ever been a time you lost sight of hope?

4. As believers, we choose to live in our hope. In what ways do we cooperate with God in order to live in our hope? Read Romans 12:2. Ephesians 4:23, Hebrews 11:1, Psalm 119:105, and Ephesians 3:16-17.

5. It has been said every person needs to know three things: to know they are loved, to know life has purpose, and to know there is hope. How does Christ fulfill all three of these needs? How has He met these needs for you?

2

HAGAR
Hope for the Forgotten

The "100 Year Flood" swept through Nashville, Tennessee, beginning in the early morning hours of May 2, 2010. Unprecedented amounts of rain quickly overwhelmed most of the city. Flooded interstate highways as well as local roads closed. Neighborhoods, malls, and churches were overcome with water. Music City had never experienced such devastating flood waters. What should have been a quiet Sunday morning became a jarring nightmare from which the city would take years to recover. I was driving that morning, heading toward Nashville on my way to Knoxville, unaware of the deteriorating circumstances ahead.

I was on the road because my college son in Knoxville was gravely ill, and I had to get to him. My husband had died just five years earlier so a sickening panic was rising in my chest—now I might lose my son. Undeterred by inclement weather, I headed out from my Illinois home early that Sunday morning, scheduled to arrive in Knoxville by midafternoon. On the way, I called a friend in Nashville, who is also a pastor, to ask him about the weather. At the time, all roads were open, and he thought I would be fine driving through Nashville. I wasn't.

My usual route through Nashville had already closed by the time I arrived. Traffic was being rerouted onto another interstate. Yet only a few miles after being rerouted, this interstate also closed because of rising flood waters. All traffic was forced to exit. I found myself in an unfamiliar part of town. My ancient flip phone had no MAPS or navigation ability. I had been in a hurry when I left home and had forgotten my car charger—now my phone had only one bar of power left. In the confusion of closing roads, my plan was to find a safe spot and wait out the storm. An abandoned gas station seemed ideal.

I parked my van under the awning, facing the street, but I watched in horror as the water continued to rise. Cars were stalling as they tried to get through the river forming in the road in front of me. I knew I was in a low lying area, but I had no idea where I was or how to get out. The panic of getting to my son now mingled with the danger of rising water. I cried out to the Lord—seriously cried out! This was no time for silent prayer. I was filled with fear and urgency. The Lord, and anyone else within earshot, was going to hear my tear-filled plea for help. Oddly, my phone rang.

It was a woman I did not know. Her pastor (my friend I had called early that morning) told her I was passing through Nashville. She had heard me speak several years earlier so she knew my story of loss. She said she was just calling to let me know she was praying for me and my son.

I blubbered, "I'm so glad you are praying for me, but right now I need more than prayers. I'm in Nashville, stuck at an abandoned gas station. I am lost and the water is rising. Please help me!"

This angel of a woman shifted into rescue mode. "Read to me the street signs. Describe everything around you."

I did.

She calmly but firmly replied, "Jennifer, you are in a flood zone. You can't stay there. You have to get out—right now!"

"My phone is about to die. I don't know which way to go. Every road is flooded." I knew my voice had an edge of fear in it.

"Stay on the phone with me, Jennifer. I own a delivery truck business. I know right where you are and I know the back roads out. Just stay on the phone—I will talk you through Nashville."

And she did!

It was a harrowing journey to be sure. She instructed me to drive up exits that were closed and proceed down the wrong side of the highway to avoid water. She knew every pothole and low spot, every turn and alley. She calmed me when I cried out in fear and she talked fast, knowing my phone was on a limited power source. Somehow, that little flip phone held its charge, and with her help I emerged on the other side of Nashville, safe from the rising floodwaters, pointed in the right direction to get to my son.

I didn't catch that dear woman's name. Although I relayed my deepest thanks to her through a later conversation with her pastor, I never talked to her again. I am confident, however, the Lord heard my cry and sent a stranger—a delivery truck owner—to guide me to safety.

Genesis tells us of another woman who is lost, filled with fear, and despairing of hope. But God sees and hears her, and He sends unprecedented help. The woman's name is Hagar.

Through her story, the Lord has much to teach us about hope.

The Character of God

Hagar is an Egyptian slave who belongs to Sarah, the wife of Abraham. Most likely, she was acquired when the patriarchal couple made their way through Egypt in Genesis 12. When reading Scripture, it is difficult to discern if Hagar is a victim, a vixen, or a villain. There are two major Old Testament passages which include her, and many other passages that include her son Ishmael (Genesis 16, 21, & 25). Additionally, the Apostle Paul refers to her in strong allegorical terms in his letter to the Galatians, giving today's New Testament readers a negative view of Hagar (Galatians 4:21-31). Regardless of how she is perceived, she is part of God's unfolding story of redemption. Even though she is a woman with many faults, none of her faults disqualify her from the mercy of God. He gives her hope in her hour of great need, and He never rescinds His promise to her. For this study, Hagar is a historical woman from an ancient time who definitely, but perhaps unknowingly, points us to Christ.

Her story is interwoven with the story of Abraham and Sarah, and it is impossible to separate one from the other. God calls Abraham to leave his home in Ur and go to a new land which God would show him (Genesis 12:1-3). God also promises to give Abraham a son who will be the heir to God's covenant promise of making Abraham into a great nation and ultimately a blessing to the entire world (Genesis 13:14-16, Genesis 15:1-6). What great promises! However, there seems to be a problem preventing God's promises from coming to fruition. Sarah, Abraham's wife, is barren.

To complicate matters further, not only is Sarah barren but neither she nor Abraham are getting any younger. The years are clicking by, and it seems God cannot deliver on His promise to give Abraham a son "from his own body." Sarah shoulders the guilt and the responsibility for seeing God's promise of a son come true. In doing so, she concocts a plan that is entirely out of step with the Lord. Sarah gives her slave, Hagar, to Abraham. The plan is for Hagar to conceive a son in Sarah's place.

To the modern reader it seems like a ludicrous plan, and yet it was not uncommon in the ancient world. Hagar would become a "slave wife" to Abraham, but because she is the property of Sarah, any children produced by Hagar and Abraham will be viewed as the children of Sarah and Abraham. To Sarah it sounds like a legitimate solution to her problem of childlessness. It sounds like a way to usher in God's promise for the sake of her beloved husband. In reality, it became one of the greatest debacles in history, the consequences of which we still experience today.

When Hagar conceives a child by Abraham, she becomes haughty (Genesis 16:4). She purposefully ignores her position as a slave and sees her fertile womb as superior to Sarah's barren womb. My sanctified imagination envisions the young beautiful Egyptian flicking her long luxurious hair over her shoulder and rubbing her round belly, taunting barren Sarah and flaunting her own successful sexual union with Abraham. Unsurprisingly, Sarah has an all-out jealous fit!

Abraham is not an innocent player in this drama. He agreed to Sarah's ill-advised plan. He indulged his desires and pleasures in the young Egyptian maid—after all his wife insisted. Sarah blames Abraham for the actions of the prideful slave. As his wife, Sarah is jealous and hurt. Children are a sign of God's favor and a husband's love. Sarah seems to have neither.

Sarah verbally lashes out at Abraham. Abraham shifts the blame right back to Sarah. Genesis 16:4-6 ripples with tension and conflict. Sin does that. This is not God's plan, and the consequences of trying to "help God" by manipulating circumstances backfires. Hagar is haughty. Sarah is jealous and angry. Abraham is indignant and confused. No one is completely innocent, and yet the brunt of all the angst is hurled onto Hagar. The Bible says, Sarah treated her harshly—and Hagar ran.

Pregnant, afraid, and alone, Hagar runs to the desert. She is running toward Egypt, 800 miles across the scorching earth. She is running to certain death, but Sarah couldn't care less. Hagar's death would end the entire fiasco. Her death would wipe the ill-fated plans from their lives so that Sarah and Abraham could start over, mend their marriage, and perhaps seek God's help. To Sarah, the death of Hagar and the death of the child in her womb would be a welcomed relief. "Let her go! Let her run! Let her die!" Hagar is a disposable commodity, no longer needed and certainly no longer valued by anyone. Yet into her seemingly dismal and worthless life…..Hope appears.

In the wilderness, beside a stream, Hagar is alone and exhausted, and Scripture says, *"Now the angel of the Lord found her…"* (Genesis 12:7). It is the Bible's first reference to the angel of the Lord. While the angel appears to others throughout the Old Testament, the *first* appearance is to a woman. *This* woman—a marginalized, throw-away slave who has no value to anyone …but God.

Most scholars agree; the angel of the Lord is the pre-incarnate Christ—Jesus before Bethlehem. The gospel of John reminds us Jesus is not only with God from the beginning, but He is indeed God (John 1:1). When Christ is born to Mary in Bethlehem, Jesus has simply taken the form of man. He is God in the flesh, God incarnate—God with skin on. But appearing to Hagar at the stream in the wilderness, Jesus is the angel of the Lord.

Genesis 16:7 rings with hope. Hagar is not looking for God. Perhaps she is familiar with the God of Abraham, but we have no indication she serves Him. Yet verse 7 clearly states, *"He found her."* Do you see it? Hagar is not looking for God, but God is looking for Hagar. In fact, He pursues her. But why?

God has made a covenant with Abraham. The covenant extends to the descendants of Abraham and Hagar is pregnant with Abraham's child. Certainly Abraham's slave marriage is not God's plan, and certainly the child conceived will not be *the* child of promise who will ultimately produce the lineage of Christ. But the child Hagar carries will be a child **with** a promise—simply because it is Abraham's child.

God is a promise-keeping God. Isaiah reminds us, *"The grass withers and the flowers fade, but the word of our God stands forever"* (Isaiah 40:8). God's adherence to His own promises is not based on human performance. His Word flows from His unchanging and faithful character. God will not abandon this child of Abraham, no matter what the circumstances. God will keep His promise to Abraham, not because Hagar is worthy but because God is faithful.

God is still a promise-keeping God. His Word stands, undeterred by circumstances, history, or human performance. There is rest in that truth for the believer in Christ. We are not free to claim anything we desire or to behave any way we choose, but we are free to lean on and live in the promises already made available to us through Christ. The promises of God are our hope, gifts of grace given to every believer. But like any gift, we must receive them, open them, use them, and apply them to our lives.

Not only does God keep His Word but also He is full of mercy and grace. God pursues Hagar because of His great compassion for her. Perhaps Hagar's reprehensible behavior makes it difficult for us to grasp God's divine compassion. But Hagar—the slave, the throw-away, the unimportant, the marginalized, and the easily forgotten—is also a victim. And God has mercy on her.

The writer of Lamentations reminds us, *"This I recall to my mind, therefore I have hope. The Lord's lovingkindnesses indeed never cease, for His compassions never fail. They are new every morning; Great is Thy faithfulness"* (Lamentations

3:23-24). I cannot argue the finer points of the doctrine of election. I cannot know for certain the eternal destiny of Hagar. Theologians have debated her place in Scripture for centuries. But this I know: the angel of the Lord, Jesus Christ Himself, stepped onto the pages of Scripture for the first time, appearing to *this* woman. I do not believe He simply appeared to her out of obligation to Abraham; rather He sees her, He knows her, He cares deeply for her, and He gives her great hope in her time of desperation.

The account of Hagar reveals to us the compassionate character of God. He is the God who pursues the lost and afraid. He is the God who loves even the unlovable. Because Christians have also experienced the goodness of God, we cannot reserve our compassion for a select few. We must follow His example and pour out the love and hope of Christ even on those who are seemingly unlovable and undeserving or those who show no propensity for meeting any standard of holiness.

If we are not careful, Christians will embrace a cold, sterile doctrine of election, which is neither presented in Scripture nor reflects the character of God. We are not called to judge the eternal destination of people. God will do that. We are called to share the gospel of Jesus Christ with a hurting, desperate, throw-away world that needs hope. Hagar is the world…and God so loved the world.

After her conversation with the angel of the Lord, Hagar refers to God by a new name, *El Roi. The God who sees me*. The spring in the wilderness is also given a new name, *the well of the Living One who sees me*. While she clearly understands the God of Abraham has stepped in on her behalf, mercifully giving her help and hope, she does not completely understand why God would intervene. However, her statements in verse 13 seem to come from a heart of gratitude and humility where there had once been pride and hopelessness.

God gave Hagar hope that day in the wilderness—and He will do the same for you. Oh, how I have run to these verses over and over in the wilderness experiences of life, clinging to the name El Roi that so beautifully reminds me of His character. God sees me. He knows me. He has compassion on me. He intervenes and gives me hope.

God is still the pursuing God. Even when we are not searching for Him, He is searching for us—not to condemn or chastise, but to offer hope. Most assuredly, the greatest hope offered is the good news of Jesus Christ. The Apostle Paul writes in Romans 5:8, *"God demonstrated His love toward us, in that while we were still sinners, Christ died for us."* Genesis 16 does not present Hagar as a seeker of God, but while she is still a sinner, an enemy of God, Jesus shows up to give hope.

God is still like that. He is not waiting for us to "get good" or clean up our lives. He pursues us in the middle of the mess when we are overwhelmed and blind to His love. If you have never met Jesus, He is offering you the hope of salvation through Christ. If you already know Him, He has not changed. He is still El Roi—the God who sees you.

Recently, I had the joy of visiting the country of Israel. A highlight of the trip was an afternoon visit to the small town of Magdala, near the Sea of Galilea. Our guide in Magdala was an enthusiastic Scottish woman named Celine. She radiated with Christ, and she was also incredibly knowledgeable of the first century synagogue uncovered in Magdala during recent archeological digs. As we viewed the recovered ruins, she explained every portion of the synagogue in remarkable detail. She showed us where students sat while the rabbi read the Scriptures. She explained the interactive dialogue that took place between the rabbis and the students. It was fascinating.

Then Celine asked our group to do more than just listen. She asked each of us to reach out and place our hand on one of the stones where ancient students would have been seated as they listened to the rabbi.

Celine gently urged, "Imagine you are a Jewish student. You have just claimed your seat in the synagogue, and today

Jesus is the visiting rabbi."

Somehow her words transported our imaginations to an ancient afternoon in Magdala as she continued, "Jesus has just read from the Scriptures and as He finishes reading, He folds the scroll—and looks up. The gaze of Christ falls upon you. What does He see?"

We could hardly breathe.

Our Scottish guide spoke with mercy, "He sees every heartache and joy. He knows everything about you. He loves you with an everlasting love and He offers hope."

As she gave her final charge, Celine's words rolled over us like fresh water on a scorching Middle Eastern afternoon, "You will take a lot of pictures here and you will buy souvenirs to take home, but I implore you to take home the gaze of Christ. It is life changing."

Hagar experienced the gaze of Christ as *El Roi*. He is the same today. He sees you. He knows you. He loves you. Listen carefully as He offers you hope.

The Circumstances of Hagar

While the Lord shows great compassion for Hagar, His compassion cannot be viewed as tolerance of sin. God addresses the sinful attitude of Hagar when He calls her "Sarah's maid," and He does not refer to her as "Abraham's wife." Genesis 16:8 is not a commentary on slavery or social justice. Scripture always reveals the character of God, and in this passage, God's righteousness and His opposition to sin is front and center. If Hagar is going to live in hope, sin must be exposed and expunged.

The angel of the Lord asks Hagar a probing, thoughtful question, *"Hagar, Sarah's maid, where are you going and where have you come from?"*(Genesis 16:8).Certainly the

Lord already knew the answer to the question, but did Hagar? It seems to be a test of sorts. Will she come to terms with her circumstances? Will she take responsibility for her role in the fiasco? Will she choose to continue running from her woes or will she face them?

Surprisingly, Hagar answers forthrightly. *"I am fleeing from my mistress Sarah"* (Genesis 16:8b). She does not blame or explain or make excuses. She states the truth, and in stating it, she acknowledges her position as a servant and Sarah's position as her master.

Remember, dear reader, this passage is not about social justice, and we cannot interpret ancient accounts through twenty-first century Western eyes. In asking her a question, God not only is getting her attention, but also dealing with sin so that hope can blossom fully. Learn from Hagar. The Lord offers us hope as well, but He will first deal with the sin that entangles us.

While running seems to be a viable option for Hagar and sometimes us—it never is. It's a fairly common response to both difficult circumstances and sin. In fact, runners are mentioned throughout Scripture—Adam and Eve, Jacob, Moses, David, Peter, and, of course, Jonah. All of these people were trying to put something behind them, trying to escape. But because God is a pursuing God of compassion, He doesn't let them run too long or get too far. He finds them and offers forgiveness and hope. He found Adam and Eve hiding in the garden. He found Jacob in Haran and Moses in Midian. God found David running back to business as usual after getting Bathsheba pregnant. He found Jonah on a ship to Tarshis and He found Peter in a fishing boat, running from his denial. In not one instance does God condone the running. He confronts it, offering hope. Submission and obedience, however, are the keys to living in the hope He offers.

When you and I come to terms with our own limitations, when we stop running from the overwhelming

WOMEN OF HOPE

circumstances of life, when we finally face who we are and how we got there—God is free to work in us. He begins to cleanse and free us, redeeming the ashes that either life or we ourselves have created. He refocuses our attention on Him and not on the sins of the past or the questions about the future. He says to us, just like He does to Hagar, *"It is time to stop running. Return and submit."*

Whoa, Jennifer! You just used the "S" word. *Submit.* Is that word really in Scripture, and if it is, surely it can't apply to women today?

Yes, the word *submit* still stands in God's Word. However, we have polluted God's intent for that word and strained its meaning through pride, culture, and our personal experience. We have lost the beauty and the security of Biblical submission.

Hagar has a choice to make. She can continue running, seemingly free, across the wilderness—and surely die there. Even if by some miracle she makes it back to Egypt, she will still be a slave, sold again to who knows what kind of master. As a slave, the baby born to her will be jerked from her womb and killed or immediately sold into slavery. There is also the slim possibility she will meet up with a group of Bedouins in the desert, but as a pregnant runaway, her plight will be dreadful in the culture of the day. Her greatest hope is to obey God and return to Abraham's household. The call to submit to Sarah is ultimately a call to submit to God's authority. In doing so, Hagar's position as a servant will not change, but her future will be secure in the hope and the promises God offers.

In returning to Sarah, Hagar is unknowingly a part of God's plan to deal with Sarah and Abraham's sin as well. Her return will force the aging couple to admit they momentarily failed to trust God. It will cause them to recognize the hurt and blame they inflicted on each other and on Hagar. Her return will remind both Sarah and Abraham to wait for the Lord's plans, in the Lord's time. Hagar's return is not just for the sake of Hagar; it is also for the child she carries and the couple she serves.

Even in our lives, the Lord does not work in a small vacuum that affects only us. Every offer of grace and hope affecting us also affects the circle of people around us. His call to submit to His authority is not to bind us; rather it is to free us and even to bless those around us. He sees farther down the road than we can see. He has a bigger picture in mind, and if we, like Hagar, will trust Him, we will live in greater freedom *under* His authority than any life we can imagine *away* from His authority.

This passage of return and submit *is not* about returning to abusive relationships. It is about facing difficult circumstances in the strength and wisdom of Christ. It encourages us to stop running, to finally and forever submit to the plans of God. We cannot fix or change other people. We cannot undo the past. But we can be obedient to whatever the Lord is instructing us to do today.

Precious reader, where have you come from and where are you going? Will you take a hard, honest look at yourself and your circumstances? Will you come to the realization that running is never the answer to lasting solutions? Will you trust the Lord Jesus who loves you and gave Himself for you? Will you trust that He has answers you cannot yet know and a future you cannot yet see? Will you lean into Him and fully surrender to His plans and His authority?

Just this morning I was reading from John 10. Jesus refers to Himself as the shepherd who lays down His life for the sheep. He also says His sheep hear His voice and follow Him. I've read that passage a hundred times but while writing about Hagar, John 10 struck me in a fresh way.

The sheep recognize the voice of the shepherd and they follow him. They do not know what road he will choose. They cannot see exactly where he is leading. They do not know what pasture they will eat from along the way or which brook will provide water. They simply trust the Shepherd and follow. They know he provides. He cares. He knows the way. Do you see it? *They are submitting to him and it is a beautiful, secure, loving relationship.* And so it is when we submit to Christ.

Remarkably in Genesis 16, Hagar believes God. She chooses life rather than death in the wilderness. God will offer Hagar hope beyond her wildest imagination, but her first response must be submission. It must be ours as well.

Where have you come from and where are you going? Trust the Shepherd. He knows the way.

The Certainty of Hope

The promise of hope given to Hagar in Genesis 16:10 is similar to the promise given to Abraham in Genesis 15:5. Not only will her unborn child live, but he will also have descendants too many to count. The promise of hope continues to flow as God instructs her to name the child Ishmael, meaning *God hears* or *God has heard.* In the naming of her child, God is reiterating His great compassion. Long after she has left the spring in the wilderness or the memory of her conversation with the angel fades, she will be reminded of the character of God every time she speaks her son's name. Ishmael. *God hears.* The God of Abraham offers hope.

While the news from the angel is not all good news, it is enough to fill Hagar with hope. She obeys the angel and returns to the household of Abraham and Sarah. In returning, not only has Hagar's sin and her fear been confronted but also Sarah's sin has been confronted. Sarah has learned to keep her hands off the plans of God. She has learned the ways and the timing of God are different from hers. Sarah is learning to wait. Hagar is learning to serve. God is doing a work in both women.

In the thirteen years that transpire between Genesis 16 and Genesis 17, Ishmael is born and grows up in the house of Abraham. Abraham loves his son as any father would. He watches Ishmael's first steps, hears his first words, and rejoices in the everyday accomplishments of Ishmael's childhood. Sarah, on the other hand, while waiting for the Lord to fulfill His promise, surely has a silent ache in her heart, a longing for her husband to love a son from her own womb. Into Abraham's contentment and Sarah's longing—God speaks.

Most of Genesis 17 is a conversation between God and Abraham. God is reminding Abraham of the covenant He has made with the patriarch. God confirms His promise of making Abraham into a great nation through whom all the world will be blessed. In the conversation, however, God reveals a new piece of information. God tells Abraham that Sarah will be the mother of this great nation (Genesis 17:16). And Abraham laughs.

Furthermore, Abraham reasons with the Almighty, questioning how an old man and an old woman can produce a child. He offers God a solution. Let Ishmael be the child of promise. Let Ishmael's descendants fulfill God's plan (Genesis 17:17-18). But God is not looking for human solutions to Sarah's dilemma of barrenness. *El Shaddai*, God Almighty, has been waiting patiently for Abraham and Sarah to come to the end of their own resources so that He alone is glorified. Sarah *will be* a mother and Isaac *will be* her son. The joyful news is bittersweet to Abraham. He has grown to love Ishmael.

The compassion and faithfulness of God are again heard as the Lord repeats to Abraham the promise He made to Hagar in the wilderness. Ishmael is indeed Abraham's son and God will not abandon this young man. The boy will become a great nation, the father of twelve princes (Genesis 17:20). God's word stands, securing Hagar's hope and abating Abraham's fears. El Shaddi and El Roi are one and the same—the promise-keeping God.

Isaac is born to Sarah when she is ninety years old and Abraham is one hundred years old (Genesis 21:1-8). The miraculous birth brings joy and laughter into the heart and home of Sarah. She cannot contain her joy and invites everyone around her to be joyful as well, giving God the glory in it all. It is no wonder Sarah is highly protective of Isaac and also highly suspicious of his older half-brother, Ishmael, the son of Hagar.

It is unclear what Ishmael does to Isaac in Genesis 21:9.Ishamel is about 16 years old at the time, a rambunctious teenager accustomed to being his father's only child. Isaac, the miracle child who has captured everyone's attention, has been weaned and is probably around three years old. Whether Ishmael is mocking Isaac, playing roughly with him, or being vulgar towards Isaac, no one knows. Whatever Ishmael does, it arouses Sarah's anger and her need to protect the only son she will ever have. Sarah demands of Abraham, "*Drive out this maid and her son, for the son of this maid shall not be an heir with my son, Isaac*" (Genesis 21:10).

Abraham is distressed by Sarah's demand, yet God comforts him. God assures Abraham of His plans for Isaac as well as His plans for Ishmael. Both are Abraham's descendants and God will not abandon either. The Lord instructs Abraham to listen to Sarah, sending Hagar and Ishmael away. What will be a difficult task for Abraham, will be earth-shattering for Hagar.

I imagine sweat drops of fear beading on Hagar's brow as Abraham packs food and water for her and her son. Her thoughts racing, "*He is really doing this! He is making us leave.*" A sense of panic seizes her as she yearns for Abraham to change his mind or lose his nerve or decide he loves Ishmael too much to see them go. But Abraham remains resolute. He gives her food and water, relinquishing his first-born son into her care and somehow trusting God with their future.

The Bible says Hagar and Ishmael wandered in the wilderness of Beersheba, an arid, mountainous region on the edge of the barren Negev desert, a place where both water and hope are in high demand. Hagar has come to the end of her understanding of hope, and the Judean sun has dried up every

46

memory of God's comforting words to her all those years ago. In dying desperation, Hagar finds shade for Ishmael and turns her back so she does not have to watch him die. Then she cries the agonizing, mournful wail of woman who has lost sight of hope.

I've been there. Losing sight of the very hope I once rejoiced in. That Sunday morning, driving through Nashville, I was a woman who lost sight of hope. I was filled with fear and dread, in part because of flood waters but primarily because I was afraid my son would die. I had momentarily forgotten the promise God gave to me twenty-one years earlier from Psalm 113:9 and the promise from Matthew 7:25 which the Lord poured into my broken heart the night of my husband's death. I had forgotten every moment of grace and mercy ever lavished on me. And when I cried out, I felt alone and forgotten under the awning of that flooding, abandoned gas station. But God would not let go. He sent a stranger, a woman on the other end of the phone, to remind me of hope.

Hope does not mean all our dreams will come true. It does not mean life will be a neat row of measurable results and quick solutions. Hope is not wishful thinking. Hope is knowing God keeps His Word. He is the promise-keeping God.

Certainly, the Lord never promises a life without pain. He never promises our children will arrive into adulthood unscathed or the lightning strike of grief will only hit once. But indeed He promises grace to meet every challenge. He promises His strength, His peace, and His presence regardless of circumstances. He promises to never leave us or forsake us. Yes, at times it feels as if life will overwhelm us. It feels as if God has abandoned us. It feels as if the promises of God will fail. But, precious reader, feelings come and go....

Hope remains.

Again, the angel of the Lord meets Hagar in the wilderness. He calls to her, asking what all the crying is about. *"What is the matter with you, Hagar?"* He implores. To Hagar, and sometimes to us, the Lord seems to say, *"Why are you living like a woman with no hope when I am still El Roi?"*

The Lord tells Hagar to lift up her son and lead him by the hand. Again, the Lord assures her of Ishmael's future, and then God opens her eyes to see an oasis which will quench her thirst as well as her fears (Genesis 21:18-19). The next verse propels the reader forward, *"And God was with the lad, and he grew; and he lived in the wilderness and became an archer"* (Genesis 21:20). Today, Ishmael is considered the father of the Arab nations, and Islam claims him as an ancestor of Muhammed. Although his descendants are still at odds with Isaac's, he remains a son of Abraham and a child with a promise. Both history and the genealogy of Ishmael in Genesis 25 confirm; Hagar's hope has blossomed.

Conclusion

There is so much doctrine and theology tied up in the account of Hagar. In his letter to the Galatians, the Apostle Paul uses the historical account in Genesis to allegorize the truth of salvation by grace. Hagar and Ishmael are representative of works and the Law in Paul's allegory. His clear and strong picture conveys the eternal truth; we cannot add to grace or accomplish by our own works what only Christ can do.

The Old Testament indeed points us to the New Testament, but we must be careful to remember the people of the Old Testament are actual people, and the events are actual historical accounts. The Old Testament as a whole is not allegory. Hagar is a real woman. Her plight is distressful and agonizing. Her sin is real. Her heartache is real. Her encounter with Christ as the angel of the Lord is real—not allegorical. It is this very real woman who captures my mind.

We cannot ignore the allegorical side of her story in Galatians 4, but we must acknowledge her humanity as well. Through Hagar's humanity, we see God revealed in truth and mercy, offering hope to an outcast and seemingly unimportant woman. Through Hagar's story, we see the Lord offering hope to people like you and me.

Dear one, some of you are wandering and crying in the wilderness of difficult circumstances. You need hope. You feel forgotten and unimportant, overwhelmed and distraught. El Roi sees you. He knows you. Just as He offered hope to Hagar when she ran from Sarah, He offers hope to you as well. The Lord is whispering to your broken heart, *"Where have you come from and where are going?"* As you ponder the answer, will you choose to face the difficult circumstances with the strength and wisdom of Christ? Will you surrender to His ways and His plan? Will you embrace the truth of His love and forgiveness? He is the promise-keeping God of Abraham and He does not dole out empty words or false hope. He loves you. He pursues you. He offers life and hope for the future through Jesus Christ. How will you respond to all He offers?

Others of us can relate to Hagar in the wilderness of Beersheba. We have lived in hope for years. We have experienced *the goodness of the Lord in the land of the living* (Psalm 27:13). We have come to imagine what our lives should look like and where they will lead. Then something unexpected happens. Life shifts. Hope seems to fade. Fear and despair crowd out our once glimmering hope and we wring our hands, forgetting the promises of God. *"Why are you living like a woman with no hope?"* The familiar voice of Christ whispers into our brokenness, redirecting our fears, reminding us He is *El Shaddai, God Almighty,* as well as *El Roi, the God who sees me.*

I carefully prayed and pondered how to bring the illustration of flooded Nashville and my ill son to a conclusion. Indeed my son survived. Eight years later, I am beaming with joy at the thought of my son, his wife, and their two darling children. God has been so good to my family. But are the tangible blessings of God where my hope lies? Do I only have hope as long as there are happy endings and joyful circumstances? Patsy Clairmont writes, "Hope doesn't announce that life is safe, therefore, we will be; instead it whispers that Christ is our safety in the midst of harsh realities" (Patsy Clairmont, *Dancing Bones, Living Lively in the Valley*).

Hope is not happy endings. Hope is not dependent on any earthly circumstance. Hope is in Christ. Everything we are in Christ and everything we have in Christ is a gift of grace—permanent, sealed, and unretractable. Even if my account of the flood and my son had ended differently, hope would remain. In death or in life, in good circumstances or bad, Christ stays the same. His promises hold true. His mercy is new every day. His strength, His peace, and His presence are available. He takes the ashes of life and somehow uses them for God's glory. He will not leave or forsake His children. He provides every need and comforts every sorrow. His salvation is eternal and victorious. Oh, there is so much available to us when our hope is in Christ. The question becomes, "Will I choose to live in the hope I have been given?"

On the night of my late husband's death, I wept and prayed for my two sons. God's tender reply was Matthew 7:25. *"And the rain descended, and floods came, and the winds blew, and burst against the house; and yet it did not fall, for it had been founded upon the rock."* A lot of storms have blown through my life and the life of my family, but not one has destroyed hope. Our hope is Christ, the foundational rock and the anchor that holds.

My hope is built on nothing less than Jesus' blood and righteousness; I dare not trust the sweetest frame, but wholly lean on Jesus' name.

When darkness seems to hide His face, I rest on His unchanging grace; In every high and stormy gale, my anchor holds within the veil.

His oath, His covenant, His blood support me in the whelming flood; When all around my soul gives way, He then is all my hope and stay.

On Christ the solid rock I stand, all other ground in sinking sand, All other ground is sinking sand.
("The Solid Rock" by Edward Mote, 1797-1874)

Are you living like a woman with no hope? Dry your eyes, precious one. Hope has come. His name is Jesus.

Discussion Questions

Read Genesis 16:1-16, Genesis 17:1-7, 15-21, Genesis 21:9-20.

1. Why did Hagar matter to God? What can we learn from this?

2. When Jesus casts His gaze upon you as El Roi, what do you think He sees?

3. God is still El Roi (the God who sees) and El Shaddai (God Almighty). One characteristic of God never diminishes, overshadows, or negates another characteristic of God. How does this bring you comfort and hope today? God cares deeply for Hagar but He does not dismiss her sin? What does this say to us?

4. The Angel of the Lord asks Hagar, *"Where have you come from and where are you going?"* How would you answer the Lord if He asked you the same question?

5. "If we will trust God, we will live in greater freedom **under** His authority than any life we can imagine **away** from His authority." How can this be true? Have you ever experienced this truth in your own life?

3

NAOMI
Hope for the Bitter

Timothy Keller writes, "Worry is believing God will not get it right. Bitterness is believing God got it wrong" (Instagram). The word *bitter* appear 36 times in Scripture. It is defined from the Hebrew in *Strong's Exhaustive Concordance* as "angry, chafed, and disappointed at being treated unfairly." *The Urban Dictionary* seems spot on in its definition. "Bitterness is often a result of a past event which has left the person hurt, scarred, or jaded" (urbandictionary.com).

All of us have experienced hurt and disappointment at times, but what pushes some souls into bitterness? How do they arrive at this undesirable place? Certainly, many of us are genuinely wounded by life's hardships. So, what prevents us from being crushed by difficult circumstances we didn't cause but have certainly been forced to carry? How does hope factor into broken or jaded lives teetering on the edge of bitterness?

I had a precious family member who lived the last two

decades of his life in bitterness. He was angry with God for the losses in his life and somehow thought his anger would ease his hurt. Instead, bitterness gnawed at his soul like a trapped coyote chewing off its own leg. My precious family member was a believer in Christ, but he died broken and bitter.

An Old Testament woman named Naomi seems to be headed in the same direction. Her name means "pleasant", but the overwhelming crush of life causes her to take up the name, Mara, meaning "bitter." What could have happened to cause such pain? Will she move through the dry valley of bitterness to emerge as a woman of hope?

Naomi's story is found in the book of Ruth. While the book is a tender and beautiful account of God's redemption, we must first wade through hardship with an older woman who has lost sight of hope. Chapter One of Ruth sets the stage. Naomi has lived many hard years. Her soul is weary, and she anticipates no relief from her troubles. *Mara* is not just her new designation; it is the cry of her broken heart.

Can you relate to her already? Keep reading. Hope is waiting.

What happened to Naomi?

The book of Ruth takes place during the time of the judges. God's people are not experiencing God's blessing. Instead, they are living in a cycle of disobedience, judgement, and finally deliverance—only to repeat the cycle soon thereafter. During the years of rebellion and disobedience, the people of God experience drought, famine, and oppression from outside enemies. During one of these cycles, a man named Elimelech decides to leave Israel and move to the land of Moab. A drought has come to his hometown of Bethlehem, and rather than starve, Elimelech choses to flee to Moab, the forbidden land of unbelievers. He takes with him his wife, Naomi, and their two sons.

While Elimelech may have initially thought their time in Moab would be brief, the Bible says, *"They remained there"* (Ruth 1:2). They make a home and settle down permanently in Moab—away from God and away from God's people. Elimelech and Naomi raise their sons in a culture which is not only foreign to them but also hostile to the ways of God. As a family, they are separated from true worship, true family, and true friendships. They are indeed surviving the drought in Israel, but in exchange, their souls become parched.

Into Naomi's already dry soul, tragedy comes. Elimelech dies, leaving her with two sons. When young men lose the voice of their father, they sometimes make rash choices. In the absence of Elimelech and as products of the culture around them, Naomi's sons marry Moabite women.

It doesn't appear these two young brides are terrible people. Even though they come from a culture that does not worship the God of Abraham, Ruth and Orpah seem to be decent women who unwittingly marry into a Jewish family. As is the tradition, the bride leaves her family and becomes the responsibility of her husband's family for the rest of her life. Ruth and Orpah join Naomi and her sons, permanently coming under one roof. Certainly, Naomi misses the security of her husband's care, but her two sons, especially the oldest, will lead the growing family. Tragedy, however, strikes again. Both of Naomi's sons die.

It wasn't her idea to come to Moab in the first place. Her husband made the choice to leave his inherited land and flee to this God-forsaken place. As a woman, she had no say in the matter. Maybe drought and impending poverty forced Elimelech's hand, but Naomi was just the submissive wife to her husband's poor choices. Certainly, she questions every decision he made for her. Perhaps she is simultaneously angry with her dead husband yet longing for his presence. Grief crushes and clouds her mind, obscuring any future and, most assuredly, any hope.

Furthermore, her grief is multiplied knowing her sons should have been her greatest blessings and her greatest assets. They should have outlived their mother, lovingly providing for her until her death. Isn't that the way things are supposed to work out? The overwhelming grief of losing her two sons is compounded by the fact that neither of her sons had children. Grandchildren would have been a tremendous blessing. They would have been next in line to care for her, carry on the family legacy, and provide leadership for the next generation. But Naomi is bereft of it all. No husband. No sons. No grandchildren. Only two daughters-in-law, unbelievers, who have left their homes and are looking to Naomi for their future.

The burden is too great for Naomi. She cannot carry the responsibility of family as well as bear the numbing gnaw of grief. The only future she can envision is poverty and ruin, shrouded in joyless existence. Tragedy has not come softly into this poor woman's life. Instead, it has beaten down the door and stolen every blessing. Where is her God? Where is her hope? My heart breaks for her.

Rumors drift through Moab that God has visited His people in Israel, ending the drought and giving them food (Ruth 1:6). Naomi decides to take her chances and return to the home of her husband's family in Bethlehem. Perhaps mercy is waiting. According to Jewish laws and customs, her daughters-in-law are now her permanent responsibility, but three widowed women without a single heir between them is the very definition of destitute.

The journey back to Israel is not a sweet and simple trip home. It is the admission of poor choices and defeat. It is the realization her fellow Israelites will be hard pressed to accept Moabite women into their midst. For Naomi, going home seems to be the admission of hopelessness and the feeling of being forsaken by God. Ruth 1:8 is a breaking point for Naomi. She cannot bear her burden another moment and tells her daughters-in-law to leave her and return to their families. Her plea to them is heart wrenching.

Go home. She begs the young women to return to their own families, remarry, have children, and be happy. She earnestly wants the Lord to bless these women because they have been kind to Naomi and faithful in their dealings with her even after their husbands died. Why would Naomi send them back since she obviously cares about these women?

Despair does that to us. It clouds our judgement. It magnifies the difficulty and blinds us to the blessings of God. Her sons could have married truly wicked Moabite women— there were plenty of them. But by giving her good daughters-in-law, somehow God is protecting and providing for Naomi long before she ever realizes it. She just can't see it or feel it in the moment; therefore, she does not believe the goodness of God. Don't be too hard on her. We do it all the time.

We judge the goodness of God based on our circumstances. If our circumstances are good, then God is good. But if our circumstances are bad, then God is bad or uncaring or unkind. We must reverse the equation. We must see God first and have a correct estimation of His character, regardless of our circumstances. The Lord is always good, always wise, always loving, and always in control, whether we see it, feel it, or even believe it. Circumstances do not dictate the character of God. Sometimes, however, that truth gets blurred by the difficulties we experience. It did for Naomi.

The first time the word *hope* is used in Scripture is Ruth 1:12. It is framed in the brokenhearted and negative words of Naomi. *"Even if I thought there was still hope for me..."* (Ruth 1:12 NIV). Naomi is referring to the ancient law of levirate marriage. If the oldest son dies without a male heir, his widow is given in marriage to the second son (or to the closest family member). The widow of the oldest son is to have a child with the second son. That child will be viewed as the child of the oldest son—inheriting the majority of the family wealth, providing for the family, and carrying on the legacy of the family.

Naomi is admitting she is too old to remarry and certainly too old to have more children. Even if she could bear more sons, there is not time for these daughters-in-law to wait for infant sons to grow up and marry them. Naomi is thinking in logical terms based on the traditions she knows. In thinking this way, she can see no future for herself or these two young women. Her despair is verbalized, *"The hand of the Lord has gone forth against me"* (Ruth 1:13). In other words—there is no hope.

While Naomi could have blamed her dead husband for all her woes, this sad verbalization seems to indicate she now views her circumstances as God's judgment for her own choices. *"This is entirely my fault and now God is judging me."* She is shouldering blame not hers to carry and feeling nonexistent condemnation because of it. She cannot yet see the goodness of the Lord in the land of the living (Psalm 27:13).

But Hope will not let go.

Naomi, Orpah, and Ruth grieve their losses together one last time. Orpah kisses her mother-in-law goodbye and walks off the pages of Scripture forever. Ruth, however, remains.

Ruth not only refuses to leave Naomi and return to Moab, but she also makes one of strongest declarations of faith in all of Scripture. Many people today use these verses in marriage ceremonies. I did. The words still move me greatly. Ruth's words convey loyalty and faithfulness to Naomi, as well as to God.

"Do not urge me to leave you or turn back from following you; for where you go, I will go, and where you lodge, I will lodge. Your people shall be my people, and your God, my God" (Ruth 1:16).

Oh, if Naomi would only open her weary heart and hear the words of hope. Unfortunately, she doesn't.

During the 30-mile walk home, she mulls her dismal circumstances and frets over her uncertain future. By the time Naomi and Ruth arrive in Bethlehem, it seems Naomi has shifted from sadness to bitterness. She seems to have moved from blaming herself to blaming God. The city is abuzz with either excitement in seeing her again or dismay at the toll life has taken. Either way, Naomi spits out her heart.

*"Do not call me Naomi [pleasant]: call me Mara [bitter], for **the Almighty has dealt very bitterly with me.** I went out full **but the Lord has brought me back empty.** Why do you call me Naomi, since **the Lord has witnessed against me and the Almighty has afflicted me?"** (Ruth 1:20-21)

Listen carefully, precious reader. It is a short trek from difficult circumstances to bitterness.

The writer of Hebrews gives a stern warning, *"See to it that no one comes short of the grace of God; that no root of bitterness springing up causes trouble, and by it many be defiled"* (Hebrews 12:15). When we allow bitterness to take root in our lives, we are denying or refusing the work of grace. Bitterness is likened to a weed. It grows quickly, sometimes overnight. It invades and eventually takes over. While a bitter person may think no one else is affected by the hazardous root, Scripture says many are affected. In fact, the people closest to us feel the effects most profoundly. God says, *"Get it out—now!"* Don't allow resentment, unforgiveness, anger, or discontent to grow, take root, and finally sprout as bitterness.

In truth, a bitter soul is an unanchored soul, untethered and moving toward disaster. Paul enumerates the progressive results of bitterness. *"Let all bitterness and wrath and anger and clamor and slander be put away from you along with all malice" (Ephesians 4:31).* Bitterness is a settled disposition that comes from a faulty perception. Left unchecked, it escalates in intensity until it explodes with malice, which is harm inflicted on another individual. To *"put away"* is a choice we make as we daily surrender to Christ and the control of His Holy Spirit. Sin always enslaves us, but God desires freedom for His children. He wants us to be free of anything that hinders the hope and abundant life that is ours in Christ.

Naomi is an unanchored soul. She *feels* as if there is no hope. Her perception of the future is skewed by the difficulties she has encountered. Indeed, life has taken a horrific toll, and an honest summation of her plight suggests none of it is a result of her personal sin. It seems Naomi has simply been dealt a bad hand, a hard life. In her grief, pain, and despair, she loses sight of hope. She allows bitterness to settle in and as Chapter One of Ruth ends, Naomi lays the blame at the feet of God.

Hope, however, begins to stir.

The Provision of Hope

"Now Naomi had a kinsman of her husband, a man of great wealth of the family of Elimelech, whose name was Boaz" (Ruth 2:1).

Ruth 2:1 is foreshadowing. The masterful writer uses a specific word, *ga al* or *kinsman redeemer,* giving the reader a taste of hopeful anticipation on the heels of the dismal events in Chapter One.

The word *kinsman or kinsman redeemer* is used 118 times in the Old Testament, and it is always used in the context of helplessness. Each time the word is used, a person, or a possession (land), is in the power of another, unable to win his/her own release. A third party must intervene to win the release of the person or to buy back the possession. The third party is the kinsman redeemer.

Leviticus 25 introduces the law of the kinsman redeemer, and according to the law, not just anyone can step in to help. There are three specific qualifications a kinsman redeemer must meet. First, he must be a blood relative of the

61

person in need. Second, he must have the ability to pay the full price of redemption. Finally, he must be willing to redeem.

Can you see it? Hope has been there all along. Naomi's plight has not suddenly put God on notice to come up with a quick solution. God has provided for Naomi's need long before she ever has a need. He put into place the law of the kinsman redeemer even before Naomi was born. He has been working on her behalf even while she blames God or misunderstands God or feels abandoned by God. Naomi's hope has always been available. It is bound to her redeemer. So is ours!

All of the Old Testament points to the New Testament. A complete reading of the book of Ruth reveals Boaz as the kinsman redeemer. He is a picture of Jesus. Boaz, however, is not the prince on a white horse rescuing the damsel in distress. Instead, he is like Christ— the gracious Redeemer, buying back the ashes of brokenness and creating something new.

Dear one, our hope is bound to Christ. He is our redeemer. He reaches into the hopelessness of sin and redeems, making us new creations (Ephesians 2:1-5, 2 Corinthians 5:17). He delivers us out of the kingdom of darkness and transfers us to His glorious kingdom of light (Colossians 1:13). Not only does He forgive and redeem the brokenness of sin, but He continues to redeem throughout our lives. He redeems the ashes of difficult circumstances, transforming tarnished ruins into something of beauty. Certainly, He is not obligated to restore everything we lose throughout our lives—but He redeems.

Furthermore, He has been here all along. Before we had a need. Before sin entered the world. Before we knew we needed a Savior. Before life took a toll. Before despair loomed. Before sickness hit. Before someone wounded us. Before it all….the Redeemer, our Hope, has been here.

As a college student, I briefly worked in Saint Louis, Missouri. One Sunday evening while attending an African-American church, I heard a message which has stayed with me for decades. The pastor spoke so eloquently and even though my frantic notes could not capture his fervor, his words still ring with hope.

"Jesus is all in all, and that is all.
He was love before love was love.
He was the door before we ever knew there was a portal to walk through.
He was the antidote before we were ever poisoned.
He was forgiveness before we ever sinned.
He was peace before there was ever conflict"
(pastor, St Louis, Missouri, 1980).

Will you see it? Christ has been our hope from the beginning (Colossians1:17).

The Realization of Hope

While hope has always been available, Naomi has not yet realized it. God, however, uses precious, industrious Ruth to clear Naomi's clouded mind.

Ruth asks to go out into the fields and glean barley so she and Naomi will have food. Gleaning is God's provision for the poor, instituted generations earlier in the Law of Moses. The Law instructs farmers to leave bits of grain on the ground for the poor to pick up or glean. Additionally, the corners of the fields are left unharvested, giving the poor an opportunity to harvest their own grain. While God makes provision for the needy, the needy must take advantage of the provision offered. Ruth is willing to glean, and Naomi gives her blessing.

The sovereignty of God is at work throughout the story of Ruth. She comes to a field that *just so happens* to belong to Boaz, the relative of her deceased father-in-law Elimelech. Boaz *happens* to spot the lovely woman and inquire about her. Boaz not only notices her, but also makes special provisions

63

for her, offering safety in his fields, meals at his table, and extra grain from his harvest. Ruth's thankfulness and Boaz' provision are the beginning of a tender relationship.

When Ruth returns home to Naomi with more grain than expected, Naomi is thrilled. She asks where Ruth gleaned that day. Ruth's response makes Naomi's head jerk! Paraphrasing Ruth 2:20, Naomi's countenance brightens, *"Huh? Boaz? I know that name. In fact, he is a relative of my late husband. A close relative. Hmmmmmm. Wait! I remember it now! The ancient law of the kinsman redeemer. Boaz could be our redeemer!"*

Naomi has just had an "Aha moment". She remembers something long forgotten. She realizes there is hope, hope which has been in place for eons. I think she genuinely smiles for the first time in months. Hope is breaking through.

Common sense will tell us we cannot remember that which we do not know. Therefore, if we are going to remember and ultimately apply the promises of God, we must already know them—before calamity strikes, before sickness comes, before disaster invades. Naomi's memory has been clouded by difficult circumstances. Either she cannot see or she refuses to see the hope God has long ago put in place for widows, orphans, and the poor. The psalmist finds himself in a similar position.

"Will the Lord reject forever? And will He never be favorable again? Has His kindness ceased forever? Has His promise come to an end forever? Has God forgotten to be gracious? Or has He in anger withdrawn His compassion?" (Psalm 77:7-9)

Have you ever felt this way? Something has shaken the writer's faith. He feels hopeless. He feels rejected. He feels as if God is not coming through. Sometimes I feel this way too! We all do. It's why we love the psalms. The writers are not only conveying their own emotions, but also conveying ours.

The psalmist, however, makes a turn. He comes to the

realization it is his difficult circumstances, not God, arousing these negative feelings. God has not changed, but hardship and grief will distort our perception of God. The writer acknowledges the source of his feelings.

"It is my grief that the right hand of the Most High has changed" (Psalm 77:10).

Scripture never invalidates feelings. God has blessed us with emotions. However, as I stated earlier in this book, feelings cannot be the rudder guiding the ship. Like the writer, we must change the way we view God. We must see Him through the lens of truth and not the emotional overflow of difficult circumstances.

"I shall remember the deeds of the Lord; Surely I will remember Thy wonders of old. I will meditate on all Thy work, and muse on Thy deeds" (Psalm 77:11-12).

When the psalmist changes his thinking, his outlook changes as well. He remembers what God has done in the past. He remembers how God has worked, not only in his life personally but also in the events of history. While we never want to live in a "good old days" mentality, it is highly profitable to recall the blessings, provision, and care we have experienced from the Lord. The blessings of the past, coupled with the truth of Scripture, become the fuel for facing our future. The remainder of Psalm 77 is a complete turnaround for the psalmist.

"Thy way, O God, is holy; What god is great like our God?" (Psalm 77:13)

When life is crushing and we become fearful, when the future is uncertain and we are overwhelmed, or when our soul needs an anchor because the waves are crashing around us, remember the Hope who anchors your soul. Remember your Redeemer. Remember Jesus.

Ah, but you must know something to remember it. If we are already believers, we know Christ more intimately by meeting daily with Him. As we meet with Him, we not only read God's Word, but also memorize it, sing it, meditate on it, and speak it back to Him in prayer. Our minds are transformed by God's Word (Romans 12:2, Philippians 4:8). As our minds are changed, our outlook is changed, and ultimately our behavior is changed. It is a process the Holy Spirit begins on the inside, and eventually, it overflows to the outside (Ephesians 3:16-19).

As we fill our minds with truth, the Holy Spirt has a well to draw from in times of duress. He uses the storehouse of our minds to point us to hope. He causes us to realize the hope already ours in Christ.

Dr. Charles L. Allen in his book, *God's Psychiatry* gives a tender illustration of recalling hope. He writes that after World War II the allied forces in Europe found hundreds of hungry, destitute, and possibly orphaned children. The children were rounded up and housed in large camps until family members could be found. While in the camps, the children were well cared for. Even though they had plenty of food, medical attention, clean clothes, and shelter, the children could not sleep. They seemed restless and afraid.

A psychologist was called in to evaluate the sleepless children. In addition to their evening meal, his solution was to give each child a piece of bread at bedtime. The bread was not for eating. It was for holding in their hands, reminding the frightened children there would be bread in the morning and the day ahead held hope. The children slept (*God's Psychiatry*).

Dear one, Jesus is our hope for tomorrow; our bread in the long, dark night of sorrow. *"This I recall to my mind, therefore I have hope" (Lamentations 3:21).* Breathe in the hope that is yours. *"Taste and see that the Lord is good" (Psalm34:8).*

The Adjustment for Hope

Now that Naomi realizes she has hope through a kinsman redeemer, she must adjust her life to live in that hope. She cannot realize her hope and then sit on her hands doing nothing. Living in hope requires faith, and faith is belief in action. So Naomi comes up with a plan.

Chapter Three of Ruth is one of my favorite chapters. I smile every time I read it. Naomi's plan is unconventional to be sure, but it is not immoral or out of step with God's design. She sends Ruth to the threshing floor where Boaz and his men are threshing grain. At night, when all is quiet, Ruth will lay at Boaz' feet and pull his covering over her. Symbolically, Ruth is asking to come under the protection and care of Boaz. She is asking Boaz to marry her.

In light of other women in Scripture, I pondered Naomi's plan. Sarah had a plan to fulfill God's promise of a son by giving her maid Hagar to her husband Abraham in order to have children through Hagar (Genesis 16). Rebecca had a plan to make Jacob the heir of God's promise by deceiving her husband and forcing the words of God to come to fruition (Genesis 27). Neither of these women did the right thing. Their plans ended in disaster. They manipulated circumstances to get selfish results. Both women failed to trust God and, consequently, acted contrary to God's ways. So how is Naomi's plan any different?

There is a difference between manipulation and participation. Living in hope requires we participate in our hope. Going back to Sarah. Once she and Abraham realized the child of promise would come from their own bodies, no matter how old they were and how impossible it seemed, Sarah and Abraham had to participate in the promise. They had to physically come together and conceive a child. Their hope for a son would have been futile if they lived in separate tents and refused to be intimate with one another. Immaculate

Conception was not an option—they had to participate!

Likewise, Naomi must participate in her hope; she must take a step of faith into the truth. She knows the law of the kinsman redeemer is God's provision for women like her and Ruth. Her plan to send Ruth to Boaz is not manipulation; it is actually trust in the provision of God. The request is made to Boaz, albeit in an unconventional manner, and then the two women get out of the way and allow the redeemer to work (Ruth 3:18-4:10).

Thankfully, Naomi is willing to adjust her life to live in her hope. She could have chosen to live out her days, grousing about her terrible circumstances and letting industrious Ruth eke out a meager existence for both of them, daily gleaning in the fields as an indigent woman. Instead, Naomi choses to live in hope, and she willingly makes changes in order to do so. Those changes include adjusting her mindset and refusing to live in the hurts of the past, turning her focus to the future and all God has in store for her family through the redeemer, and waiting with anticipation for God to fulfill His promise— rejoicing in the outcome.

Living in hope requires us to adjust our lives and participate in our hope. What adjustments must you make in order to live in the hope that is yours through Christ, the Redeemer?

Is there a sin to confess or an attitude to forsake? Do you need to let go of a hurtful past and embrace the Lord's mercy and grace? Do you need to forgive someone who has wronged you? Is there a secret habit or an unhealthy relationship you should release? Is there a mindset or thought process that must be captured and transformed?

Hope is always forward facing. We are to move ahead, walking obediently day by day, anticipating with confidence the promises of God. To live obediently requires adjustments from time to time. We make these adjustments based on the Word of God and with the strength of the Holy Spirit living within us (Philippians 2:13). Adjustments are not a "do better, try harder" mentality. Adjustments are a response of faith while trusting God to work.

Naomi is finally looking to the Lord for her future. She is no longer looking back at her dismal past. The Apostle Paul writes, *"Forgetting what lies behind and reaching forward to what lies ahead, I press on..." (Philippians 3:13-14a).* Paul is not suggesting amnesia. He is, however, urging us to look ahead, to continue moving forward, and to refuse being enslaved by our past. Isaiah says it this way:

"Do not call to mind the former things, or ponder things of the past. Behold, I will do something new, now it will spring forth; will you not be aware of it? I will even make a roadway in the wilderness, rivers in the desert "(Isaiah 43:18-19).

Hope is ours in Christ. The question is, will we make the necessary adjustments to live in it?

The Fullness of Hope

The book of Ruth ends quite differently than it began. Ruth marries Boaz and a son, Obed, is born to them. This young life is considered the firstborn son of Ruth's late husband. As the firstborn son, Obed will inherit the wealth of Boaz, the family name, the family land, and the responsibility to continue the family legacy. Boaz, as well as Obed, will be Naomi's security for the future. Her family now has the means to care for her until she dies. The child is also her assurance Elimelech's line will continue. In fact, Obed will be in the lineage of King David and ultimately the lineage of Christ. Certainly the Lord has greatly blessed Naomi through a kinsman redeemer. Her heart is full to overflowing. Mara is no more.

Naomi's joy is not based on the false pretense that nothing bad will ever happen again. She knows trials may come again. She understands difficulties may someday be a part of life again. She is not naïve or ignorant about the future possibilities of sickness, grief, or death. Yet she is still joyful! Why? Because she has hope.

Naomi is looking forward with new eyes of anticipation. God has supplied her needs in abundance; He will not abandon her in the future. Her circumstances no longer toss her about like a ship in a storm because her soul is now anchored. The redeemer has come bringing hope, and peace, and joy to her heart. And oh, her joyful hope is evident through her countenance, her actions, and her words.

Read carefully Romans 15:13.

"May the God of hope fill you with all joy and peace, as you trust Him, so that you may overflow with hope by the power of the Holy Spirit" (NIV).

A friend of mine once said, "Hope, joy, and peace are like best friends. They go everywhere together. If we have one, we have the other two as well." As we trust the God of hope, He fills our lives with joy and peace which overflow in hope. All three characteristics are evidence of the Holy Spirit working in us. They are not byproducts of blissful, problem-free days. Instead, they are most profoundly evident in the tough days when problems seem to multiply. While the Holy Spirt is always working, our responsibility is to trust Him.

I grew up in a pastor's home. My father was my only pastor until I left home to attend college. He was not only a good pastor but also an excellent preacher, a masterful story teller who could illustrate Biblical principles like no other. I still remember many of his sermon illustrations I heard as a child.

My dad had a gift for words. He wrote and spoke them eloquently. He liked crossword puzzles and word games. He had a Master's degree in Speech Pathology and helped many students overcome diction and pronunciation problems. He was a stickler for correct grammar and enjoyed etymology. He had a brilliant mind and communicated his thoughts concisely and articulately. However, a massive stroke in 2012 changed everything.

My once communicative father was not only paralyzed on his dominant right side, but all forms of communication were disrupted as well. In addition to being bedridden, he could no longer speak, read, or write. His bright blue eyes conveyed understanding, but he could utter only one word, *"Wonderful."*

My 81-year-old mother took care of my father at home, in this condition, for twenty-two months. She was a picture of loyalty and tenacity, and he was a picture of patience and love. On the days I was in town, I watched my mom hoist my father out of bed each morning with a hydraulic lift, lower him into a wheelchair, and wheel him to the breakfast table so he could eat at the table instead of in the bed. Unfortunately, it took hours to eat the breakfast she lovingly prepared. His awkward left hand and his useless right hand seldom cooperated. Food went everywhere, caught only by the childlike bib around his neck.

"Honey, do you want peaches or blueberries this morning?" my mother called to him knowing full well what his answer would be.

"Wonderful," my sweet daddy responded.

"Ok, dear, blueberries coming right up," she cheerfully responded.

After a laborious breakfast, the conversation continued.

"Sweetheart, would you like to sit outside in the sunshine for a few minutes?"

"Wonderful," he gently replied.

As he grew weary from the morning's events, my mom would roll the wheelchair back to the hydraulic lift, attaching the four corners of a sling positioned underneath my dad to the lift. She would pump the lift's handle, suspending my dad in mid-air until he was clear of the wheelchair. Never pausing, she pushed the heavy lift and my dangling father toward his bed, gently lowering him into the hospital bed by the living room piano.

The insidious stroke robbed my dad of every human dignity. My mother graciously cared for each ability he lacked. She worked tirelessly, and he always responded with "*Wonderful.*" For twenty-two months.

It was Thanksgiving, almost a year into dad's stroke. The family had gathered in my parent's home. Children and grandchildren were everywhere. We all helped with the morning ritual of getting my daddy to the breakfast table. My sister and I prepared a big breakfast. The entire family held hands to say a blessing on that Thanksgiving morning when my mother shocked us all.

She turned to my silent dad and asked, "Sweetheart, would you like to say the blessing for us this morning?"

How could she do that? It irritated me—humiliating my wordless dad with the job of praying—especially with so many of us gathered on this special Thanksgiving morning. He might say "*wonderful*" and then most assuredly, he would fall into the unintelligible mumbling we were accustomed to. How could she ask such a thing?

He replied to her jarring question with a smile, "*Wonderful.*"

We all bowed our heads and closed our eyes, waiting on the inevitable. Instead, something miraculous happened.

Clearing his throat, my daddy began to pray with a clear mind and a resonant voice. He articulately spoke three words.

"Thank you, Lord."

And then he fell into the familiar mumbling. Every eye opened as he mumbled the rest of his prayer. Every mouth agape. Tears streaming down most of our faces. We had just heard the greatest sermon our dad had ever preached.

I often wonder, if the Lord gave each of us an opportunity to speak only three words to Him during our greatest suffering, what would those three words be?

"Why me, Lord?"
"How could You?"
"You should have…."
"Don't you know…?"
"Please change this!"
But not many of us would say, "*Thank you, Lord.*"

My precious, stricken father spoke words of thankfulness in his darkest days. Why? Because he had hope. And in having hope, he also had joy and peace when everything else in his life had been stripped away. My dad knew the Lord had not abandoned him and never would. He knew Christ would give him the grace and strength to meet each day no matter what the day held. He knew he had been blessed with countless blessings. He knew no matter the outcome of this life, heaven was his final home. My father knew and experienced the fullness of hope, even in the difficult days. He chose to live in his hope.

Dear reader, hope is yours as well. Will you see it? Will you adjust your life to live in it? Will you trust the Lord, allowing His Holy Spirit to do a work in you evidenced by joy, peace, and overflowing hope?

Difficult circumstances temporarily blinded Naomi to hope. They can blind us as well. Like Naomi, we can wander dangerously close to permanent bitterness. But hope does not give up and let go. It has been available from the beginning. Naomi realized her hope and adjusted her life to live in the fullness of it. Will you? Your hope is Christ. He is the anchor for your soul. Let go of Mara. Embrace your hope.

Discussion Questions

Read the Book of Ruth

1. What kind of mental picture do you get when the Bible refers to bitterness as a root? What kind of damage can bitterness do in a family or a church family? Read Hebrews 12:14-15. How does verse 14 help us live out verse 15?

2. As we examine the story of Naomi, how can we avoid the pitfalls of bitterness—even when life is difficult and seemingly unfair?

3. How was Naomi's plan in Ruth 3:1-4, different from Sarah's plan in Genesis 16:1-4? Sometimes as women, we are guilty of manipulating circumstances and pretending it is the Lord at work. What is the difference between trusting/cooperating with God's plans and coming up with our own plans to "fix" things? How can we know the difference?

4. When life is difficult and we lose sight of hope, where can we turn? Read Psalm 116:1, Psalm 119:18, 28,105, Psalm120:1, 1 Thessalonians 5:11.

5. How can we be thankful, living anchored in our hope, when circumstances are overwhelming? Read James 1:2-4, Romans 8:28, Jeremiah 29:11, Jeremiah 33:3, Psalm 62:5-8,

4

HANNAH
Hope for the Praying

"I strongly suspect that if we saw the difference even the tiniest of our prayers make, and all the people these prayers affect, and all the consequences of these prayers down through the centuries; we would be so paralyzed with awe at the power of prayer, we would be unable to get up off our knees for the rest of our lives" (Peter Kreeft, Professor of Christian Apologetics and Philosophy at Boston College).

Prayer is one of God's greatest gifts to believers in Christ. Yet it seems to be a gift for which we are thankful, but rarely use. Like so many other blessings, we have mystified prayer. We have relegated it to the eloquent, the bold, the knowledgeable, the professionals, or perhaps the celebrities of the faith. But prayer is for every believer. God uses our prayers to accomplish His will on earth. Through prayer, we have been given the privilege of participating in the plans of God. Hannah is a woman who prayed—for years. We will glean much from her account framed within the context of prayer. However, as is true with all of Scripture, this is God's story. Indeed, He uses human lives and human events to reveal Himself, His character, and His plans, but make no mistake— God is central in all of Scripture. He is central in the story of Hannah as well.

A cursory reading of First Samuel 1 will lend itself to a faulty and certainly limited view of prayer. It will lead us to believe Hanna desired to have a son, she prayed, God answered, and Samuel was born. This one-dimensional approach, however, makes Hannah the central figure, struggling with God in prayer until she gets her way. We cannot view prayer as a wrestling match with God.

Likewise, we cannot limit eternal God to answering only finite prayers. He is not a cosmic genie, waiting to grant our every wish. Neither can we imagine Him as resistant to or negligent of our needs when He willingly supplies every need. We must change our perception of prayer and view it from God's perspective. Jennifer Kennedy Dean writes, "Prayer is the means by which we are freed from our earthbound thinking to participate in eternity" (Jennifer Kennedy Dean, *Live a Praying Life*).

As the book of 1 Samuel begins, two truths are simultaneously presented. Both of them are equally important to Almighty God.

First, the nation of Israel has a need for a spiritual leader, and God has a divine plan to give them one. His people are walking in spiritual darkness, caught in the cycle of rebellion, judgement, deliverance, and finally obedience—only to repeat the cycle.

At the core of their spiritual darkness is corrupt spiritual leadership. Eli is the high priest, and his two sons, Hophni and Phinehas, also serve as priests. The Bible is crystal clear. *"Eli's sons were wicked and had no regard for the Lord"* (1 Samuel 2:12). In fact, they are shamelessly wicked and everyone knows it. Their father Eli does little, if anything, to correct them (1 Samuel 2:22-25). The wickedness of Phinehas and Hophni prevent the people from hearing God's voice (1 Samuel 3:1), and eventually the Lord tells Eli both his sons will die on the same day. In their place God will raise up a faithful priest *"who will do according to what is in My heart and mind"* (1 Samuel 2:35).

The second truth simultaneously presented in 1 Samuel is more personal and perhaps more relatable to us. It is Hannah's deep, heartfelt, even brokenhearted desire to have a child.

The connecting point of these two truths is the prayers of Hannah. God has a plan for Israel. Hannah has a need. In His divine wisdom, God will use *her prayers* to set into motion *His plans* while also meeting *her need.* Only the Almighty, Sovereign God could orchestrate such a thing.

A question, however, comes to mind. If God is going to carry out His divine, sovereign plans anyway, why should we pray?

With or without us, God is sovereign. However, He is a relational God who invites His children to be part of the process. His invitation for us to participate in His plans, through the means of prayer, does not in any way diminish His ability or His authority. He has simply chosen to carry out His heavenly purpose here on earth through intercessors. "When God wants to change the course of events, He calls out an intercessor. Prayer opens the way for God to do what He longs to do" (Jennifer Kennedy Dean, *Live a Praying Life*). The Lord has much to show us about hope and prayer. He uses Hannah's difficult circumstances and her deepest desires to reveal His own heart, pointing us toward hope.

Pray Related

Hannah is an ordinary Jewish woman living during the time of Judges with her husband Elkanah in the city of Ramah. Unfortunately, she is not Elkanah's only wife. Polygamy is evident in Scripture for a short time early in Israel's history. It was never God's intention for marriage, and when it is presented, there is always trouble. Peninnah is the other wife. She is a contentious, persistent thorn to Hannah. The problem is simply stated, *"Peninnah had children, but Hannah had none" (1 Samuel 1:2).*

Every year, Hannah goes with her husband to worship the Lord at Shiloh where the tabernacle is located. It seems that neither Hannah nor Elkanah are caught in the web of idolatry and wickedness that permeates much of Israel during this time. They are worshippers, rightly related to Yahweh because of His covenant with Israel. Even as a woman in a patriarchal culture, Hannah has the right and the privilege to worship and pray because she has a relationship with God.

As Christians, we too are blessed with the right and the privilege to pray. But we do not approach holy God on our own merit. Jesus says, *"I am the way, and the truth, and the life. No one comes to the Father except through me "(John 14:6 NIV).* A relationship with Christ is required to come into the presence of God.

When the disciples ask Jesus to teach them to pray, Jesus instructs them to pray in this way, *"Our Father who art in Heaven..."* (Matthew 6:9-13). The words, *Our Father* indicate a relationship. It is an exclusive relationship. Not everyone can call Him Father—only those who know Christ. The phrase *Our Father* is also inclusive. In using the plural pronoun *our,* Jesus is letting us know we are part of a family, and we are not God's only child.

Recently, I visited the Billy Graham Library in Charlotte, North Carolina. Listening to an archived sermon by the late evangelist, I was struck anew by the simplicity of the gospel and the uncomplicated manner with which Billy Graham presented transformational truth. Today it seems our quest for intellectualism has made the simple truth of salvation an obstacle course of theological jargon. And yet...the truth remains simple:

We are all sinners, separated from God. But God loves us with a great love and chose to send His only son, Jesus Christ, to die on a cross as payment for our sins. We respond to God's gift of His Son by confessing we are sinners, asking Jesus to forgive us, and receiving Him as the Lord of our lives. Knowing Christ makes us rightly related to God. It makes us part of God's family and gives us access to prayer. Because of Christ, we can partake in the marvelous invitation of Hebrews 4:16, *"Let us therefore draw near with confidence to the throne of grace, that we may receive mercy and may find grace to help in time of need."*

The privilege of praying, whether under the Old Covenant or the New Covenant, is based on God's grace extended to sinful people. The throne of grace is not exclusively a New Testament concept. Certainly, we have a better understanding of grace in light of God's complete revelation through Christ, but prayer has always been about grace. Gracious God is listening to the prayers of Hannah just as He does ours. As in Hannah's story, something is stirring; God has a plan yet to unfold. We pray rightly related—waiting, anticipating with hope the goodness of God.

Pray Aligned

Hannah is praying for a son. Because Elkanah has children with Peninnah, Hannah is certain the problem of childlessness lies within her. Her heartbreaking prayer has gone up to God for years. So why hasn't God answered? What could God be waiting for? A close study of 1 Samuel 1:7-11 gives insight into God's timing as well as Hannah's praying.

Because of her great sadness, Elkanah tries to comfort his precious Hannah. But his words are almost humorous to any woman who has longed for a child. He consoles her by asking if he is not better than ten sons. He seems to say, "Can't I be enough to soothe your troubled heart, Hannah?" Elkanah's good intentions only drive Hannah further into desperation. In her distress, her praying takes a serious turn.

Hannah has prayed to be a mother for years, but verse 11 changes everything. She is willing to have a son who is totally dedicated to the Lord and to the Lord's plans. In the past, Hannah has simply prayed for a son. Now, she is praying for the prophet and leader God longs to give. Within the year, God answers Hannah's prayer. *God responds to Hannah when her prayers align with His plans.*

Augustine of Hippo explains, "Prayer is not merely expressing our present desires. Its purpose is to exercise and train our desires so that we want what He is getting ready to give us. His gift is very great, and we are very small vessels for receiving it. So prayer involves widening our hearts to God."

Jesus taught His disciples to pray, *"Thy Kingdom come. Thy will be done on earth as it is in heaven"* (Matthew 6:10). Likewise in His final message to the disciples, Jesus says, *"Until now you have asked nothing in my name. Ask and you will receive, that your joy will be made full"* (John 16:24). We can't just run with the idea of asking for anything we desire. We must pray through the lens of His will and His kingdom. To do this, we ask—we pray—in Jesus' name. But what does that mean? And how do we do it?

While many times the phrase *in Jesus' name* is dutifully tacked on to the end of sincere prayers, it is not a phrase that somehow seals the deal and obligates God to answer well-intentioned prayers. In fact, speaking the words *in Jesus' name* is not even necessary when we pray. Read the Lord's Prayer. You won't find that particular grouping of words. You will, however, find the essence of the phrase. Two general principles help explain the phrase *in Jesus' name*.

1. We are rightly related to God through Jesus.
2. We are rightly representing the desires of Jesus.

We have already discussed being rightly related to God through Christ, but additionally, our prayers must also reflect the desires of Christ. Our prayers must represent Jesus' concerns— the things Jesus Himself would pray about. These two principles guard us from rogue praying, conceived in selfish, ignorant, or naïve desires. Praying in Jesus' name places our focus on the heart of God, making His plan and His purpose central.

God's Word is always the plumb line for our prayers. Jesus makes it clear, *"If you abide in Me and My words abide in you, ask whatever you wish, and it shall be done for you" (John 15:7)*. Again, we cannot separate the first half of the verse from the second half. We cannot simply ask for whatever we wish and expect God to come through. Praying in this way is presumptuous and will only lead to disappointment and resentment. The solution, however, is *abiding*.

Abiding *in* Christ directs our asking *from* Christ. When we abide in Christ, we are allowing Him to permeate every part of us. Likewise His Word, His principles, His instructions, His standards, and His teaching permeate our hearts and minds as well. We become soaked and saturated with the things of Christ, thus changing our desires. *Abiding* changes the way we pray.

Psalm 37:4 confirms the New Testament principle of *abiding*. *"Delight yourself in the Lord; and He will give you the desires of your heart."* Again, keep the two phrases together. We cannot anticipate receiving the unfettered desires of our heart without understanding the transformational truth of *"delight in the Lord."*

The Hebrew word for *delight* has nothing to do with happiness. Instead, it means "to conform" or "to be pliable." When we are pliable in the Lord's hands, He conforms us to His image. He changes us from the inside out, and consequently our desires change as well. When our desires match God's desires, He is free to give us our heart's desire.

We test the integrity of our desires by the Word of God. The Lord will NEVER do or give anything contrary to His Word. Our praying must always line up with Scripture and rightly represent the heart of Christ.

Additionally, the Holy Spirit guides our praying, always using the Word of God. Jesus comforts His disciples in the Upper Room by telling them a Helper is coming. *"When He, the Spirit of truth comes, He will guide you into all the truth...* "(John 16:13). Jesus clarifies *truth* when he prays, *"Sanctify them [set them apart] in the truth; Thy word is truth" (John 17:17).* The Spirit and the Word align us to the will of God so that we are praying about the things God already wants to do.

I have been a systematic Bible reader for years. I use devotional material from Scripture Union, a Bible reading ministry located in Pennsylvania (scriptureunion.org). Each day, their printed material gives me direction as I read, reflect, study, and pray through a small passage of Scripture. By using the Scripture Union devotional guide over a span of five years, every major passage in the entire Bible is covered—even the hard stuff, like Leviticus! Through the years I have discovered a wonderful principle: God speaks through His word—all of it—even the passages I would typically avoid.

Each day before I ever read a single verse of Scripture, I make a list of people, problems, and events that are on my mind—things that concern me. Then I read the designated passage of Scripture. I meditate on it. Mull over it. Even question it sometimes. After reading, I ask the Lord to apply that particular passage of Scripture to my list of concerns. It is amazing how God's Word—even the difficult and obscure passages—speaks to my list. Furthermore, the Holy Spirit uses the verses I have just read to guide my praying about the concerns I have written.

This system works well for me, transforming my daily time with the Lord from dusty duty to vibrant relationship. I anticipate hearing His voice. I am thrilled to know He hears my concerns and He is at work, sometimes behind the scenes, waiting for His timing to unfold. Allowing the Holy Spirit to use God's Word assures me I am rightly representing the heart of Christ as I pray through my concerns for the day. However, if any adjustment needs to be made in my thoughts or attitude, the Holy Spirit is quick to convict, almost always using the verses I have just read.

Equally amazing is the Holy Spirit's reminder throughout the day of all I have experienced in those quiet moments with Him. When doubts or troubles arise during the day or my concerns come crashing back in the form of fretting or worry, I can recall His Word, His presence, and His promises. I can breathe a prayer as I go about my day, continuing to take my concerns to Him.

But how does this pertain to Hannah? She did not have the entirety of Scripture neither the indwelling of the Holy Spirit. So how did God direct her praying to finally align with His will? What caused Hannah to pray for the very thing God already wanted to give?

God used her difficult circumstances to align her prayers with His will.

The Lord used Hannah's barrenness. He used the goading of Peninnah. He used the years that passed. He used the yearning of Hannah's heart. He used all of these things to press her into praying for a child totally and completely dedicated to the Lord's service and the Lord's purpose. Hannah's prayer in 1 Samuel 1:11 is not a bargain with God. Rather it is evidence of Sovereign God at work in her life, raising up an intercessor who will beseech the Lord for the very thing He wants to provide.

This is a tough truth for us to swallow. We like instant answers. We enjoy the still waters and green pastures of life. We desire ease and pleasure. We want God to fix or change every difficulty that arises when in actuality, everything in a believer's life works together for the purposes of God. Even our hardships and heartaches.

God will use our heartaches to direct our praying. Certainly, God's Word remains the plumb line for our prayers, and His Holy Spirit remains the energy and the guide. But our deepest desires, our most difficult circumstances, and our greatest hurts drive us—they press us into prayer.

When I remarried in 2006, I gained three wonderful step-children. Our family has long since dropped the term *step,* and I view my additional three as the children God grafted into my heart. Remarriage and the blending of two grieving families, however, was no easy task. There was turmoil and strife and disagreements and heartache. God graciously used it all to direct my prayers.

Instead of praying for good grades in school or happy days at home, I grabbed Colossians 1:9-12 and began praying fervently for each child. I prayed for God to do a work in our turbulent home and, subsequently, in each child. My prayers were guided by Paul's prayer for the church in Colossi. My heartache pressed me into praying for things higher than my own desire for comfort. Today, twelve years later, my five children are still a work in progress. However, each of them is also an extraordinary testimony of grace.

Hannah never would have prayed for a prophet and a servant devoted to the Lord had God quickly answered her initial prayer. She never would have been desperate enough to surrender her plans and embrace the Lord's plans. God wanted a Samuel. Hannah just wanted a son. But in His love and sovereignty, God allowed dear Hannah to be pressed, aligning her desires with His.

God's wonderful answer changed Hannah's life forever, but it also changed the nation of Israel. Hannah received a son, and the nation gained a great spiritual leader who led them out of spiritual darkness. Samuel was God's answer both for Hannah and for Israel. Only the Lord could design such a plan.

Do you see it? God has chosen to work through the prayers of His people. He has chosen to use all things, even heartache, for His purpose. Prayer is not overcoming God's reluctance. It is laying hold of God's willingness. It is letting go of our limited agenda and embracing the plans of God. There is great hope when we pray aligned.

Does praying aligned mean we must use perfectly worded prayers? Absolutely not! When Eli the priest meets Hannah, he thinks she is drunk. Her lips are moving, her heart is breaking, her tears are flowing, but no words are spoken. Make no mistake, she is indeed praying. She is *"speaking in her heart, only her lips were moving, but her voice was not heard"* (1 Samuel 1:12-13).

John Bunyan, author of *Pilgrim's Progress,* wrote, "When we pray, God infinitely prefers a heart without words to words without heart." Sometimes our prayers come from deep distress, deep pain, or even deep confusion and fear. Expressing ourselves, even in prayer, is often limited by the very language we speak. We have no words. But God does. Paul writes in Romans 8:26 about the blessed hope we have when words fail us. The Holy Spirit, the Helper, intercedes for us. He transposes our wordless praying into intelligible concerns before the Lord's throne of grace and mercy.

All of us have or will experience this depth of heartache and concern. As believers in Christ, however, we can rest in God's promise; the Holy Spirit is at work on our behalf. In Romans 8, The Apostle Paul is not referring to an unintelligible tongue, an altered state, or a prayer language; rather he is offering hope to the broken. God hears the prayers of His children, even when we have no words.

Can we always know the perfect will of God when we pray? In my opinion, no we cannot. Hannah began praying for a child who would be dedicated to the Lord, but she could not see the future. She did not have a complete understanding of all God would do through her dedicated son. For us, God's Word and the Holy Spirit give us direction, and our abiding in Christ changes our desires. But we do not always see clearly the path of God's will. Even Jesus prayed and then relinquished His will to the will of the Father. *"Not my will but Thine be done"* (Luke 22:42). There is no shame in praying as closely aligned to God's will as we are able and then releasing all things into God's hands. Releasing is evidence of a surrendered life. My family friend the late Dr. Wayne Barber described prayer as "the verbalization of a surrendered life." It is this surrendered life that prays even when there is little understanding of God's will or God's ways. We pray anyway—and leave it to Him to respond however He chooses.

Praying aligned takes practice. It is part of *"working out your salvation"* (Philippians 2:12), learning to live in all that is ours in Christ. Effective praying requires an inner transformation and daily abiding—a heart and mind centered on Christ. The purpose of praying aligned is not to gain what we desire, but it is to reflect the heart of Christ.

Pray Cleansed

Sin is the greatest deterrent of prayer. It clouds our spiritual senses. It dulls the voice of God in our lives. It quenches and grieves the indwelling Holy Spirit. We typically avoid God's Word when sin is ongoing, and consequently, we cannot clearly understand the desires of God. If we are to pray effectively, we must allow the Lord to deal with personal sin. Elkanah, Hannah's husband, is a Levite. Occasionally, he would be called to serve in the tabernacle in Shiloh, but

Elkanah is also devout in taking his entire family to Shiloh once a year to worship. This annual trip to the tabernacle includes offering sacrifices as prescribed by the Mosaic Law (1 Samuel 1:3). For any Israelite, the most important of all occasions is the Day of Atonement, the holiest day when sacrifices are made for the sins of the people (Leviticus 23:26-28). A few days later, it is followed by a joyful celebration during the Feast or Festival of Booths. The annual pilgrimage to Shiloh by Elkanah and his family is most likely the observance of the Day of Atonement and the feasts that follow.

Elkanah is a righteous man. He leads his family to be in a right relationship with Holy God, cleansed of sin. Hannah participates. Every year. She refers to herself as a *"handmaiden of the Lord,"* surrendered to His service and obedient to His laws (1 Samuel 1: 11). Sin is not a deterrent to Hannah's prayers.

It is interesting to note that in addition to being rightly related to Holy God, Hannah is also rightly related to other people. Throughout the entire account, Hannah does not speak a single word of accusation to Elkanah. She does not blame him for her distress or ridicule him for taking a second wife. She endures with patience, though with heartache, the goading of Peninnah. There is not a single recorded word of backlash or anger towards the divisive, arrogant second wife. Hannah even patiently endures the harsh words of Eli, accusing her of being drunk. As she explains her dilemma to the high priest, there is no hint of anger or insult in her reply to him.

Her relationship with God has an effect on her relationship with people. Ours does too.

If sin gets a foothold in our lives, it quickly affects our relationships, especially those closest to us. Sin dulls our spiritual senses and consequently everything about us which is Christ-like dulls, diminishes, or disappears. Mercy, grace, forgiveness, kindness, peace, joy, discernment, wisdom...and prayer are adversely affected by sin.

James 5:16 states, *"The effective prayer of a righteous man can accomplish much."* The word *effective* means "specific." A righteous person, praying specific prayers, accomplishes a lot in the kingdom of God. The key, however, is the word *righteous.*

When we come into the family of God, we are given the righteousness of Christ. It is a miraculous exchange, our filthy unrighteousness for His perfect righteousness. We do not just HAVE righteousness; we ARE righteous in the sight of God. Our position has changed. We are no longer slaves to sin, living under the domain of darkness. Instead, we are children of God, clothed in the righteousness of Christ, transferred to His kingdom of light. We are positionally right with God because of Christ (2 Corinthians 5:21, Colossians 1:13-14).

Since our position has changed, our practice or our lifestyle must change as well. We must practice righteousness, and it is the Holy Spirit within us who enables us to live as God has commanded us to live. We ARE righteous; therefore, we must LIVE righteously (Ephesians 3:16-19, Philippians 2:13).

Prayers are hindered when practical, daily-living righteousness is ignored. James 4:3 doesn't mince words. *"You ask and do not receive because you ask with wrong motives...."* Our motivation for praying—along with our desires, our needs, and our expectations—will be skewed when sin is present.

But as always, there is hope.

"If we confess our sin, He is faithful and righteous to forgive us our sin, and cleanse us from all unrighteousness" (1 John 1:9). It is just so simple! While sin wants *to keep us from God*, the invitation is to *run to God*—confessing anything that hinders our relationship with Christ, anything that obstructs our prayers, anything that harms those we love, anything that casts a shadow on the goodness of God. Confessing is not

giving the Lord new information. He knows everything about us. Confession is agreeing with God about the sin He is already aware of. When we confess, He not only forgives us but also cleanses us, washing away the grime of sin that messes up everything…even our prayers.

The Psalmist has it right. *"Search me, O God, and know my heart; Try me and know my anxious thoughts; and see if there be any hurtful way in me, and lead me in the everlasting way"*(Psalm 139:23-24). Dear reader, God uses His Word and the Spirit of Christ within you to search you and try you, revealing all the things that need to be confessed and forsaken. For me, searching and trying my thoughts, my motives, and my actions is a daily exercise, sometimes even hourly.

Prayer is the greatest work we will ever do. Sin affects prayer. Pray cleansed, dear one, pray cleansed.

Pray Thankful

Hannah's joy cannot be contained. God has blessed her with a son whose name is Samuel (1 Samuel 1:20). Because my late husband and I prayed for several years to have a child, Hannah's words to Eli in 1 Samuel 1:26-28 are especially meaningful to me.

"Oh, my lord! As your soul lives, my lord, I am the woman who stood here beside you, praying to the Lord. For this boy I prayed, and the Lord has given me my petition that I asked of Him. So I have also dedicated him to the Lord; as long as he lives he is dedicated to the Lord."

Then Hannah prayed…….

The second chapter of 1 Samuel bursts forth with a jubilant and thankful prayer from the heart and lips of Hannah. Her song of thanksgiving. Although her song is filled with moving praise, it is not the beginning of her thankfulness.

When Hannah first encounters Eli, she dispels the notion she is drunk, painfully articulating her desires to have a son. Eli listens and then encourages her. After his encouragement, her heart is settled, thankful, and hopeful (1 Samuel 1:18). She is confident the Lord has heard her cries. Her appetite returns. Her countenance brightens. She worships God the next morning. No tears. No pleas. Just quiet anticipation. Hope.

While we expect Hannah to overflow with joy after Samuel is born, we often miss the fact she is thankful before he is born. She is filled with joy and peace while she waits, while she anticipates, while she hopes in the Lord. We are encouraged to do the same.

"Be anxious for nothing but in everything by prayer and supplication with thanksgiving, let your request be made known to God, and the peace of God, which surpasses all comprehension, shall guard your hearts and your minds in Christ Jesus" (Philippians 4:6-7).

Paul is admonishing Christians to pray instead of worry. He is encouraging us to make our requests known to God, but with an underlying truth we often neglect. He tells us to make our requests with thanksgiving—being thankful *before* we see God's answer. While we usually express our thanks after the fact, Paul is teaching us to be thankful in anticipation of God's response. Be careful. We are not *claiming* answers before they come and somehow obligating God to give us what we want. Instead, a thankful heart simply proves we are trusting God, no matter how He chooses to respond to our need—even if He says *no* or *wait*.

While we rejoice with Hannah in the birth of Samuel, we also understand there is great sacrifice in her answered prayers. When Samuel is around three years old, firmly embedded in the heart of his mother, Hannah and Elkanah take him to Shiloh. After worshipping the Lord, the couple returns to Ramah, leaving their precious son with Eli (1 Samuel 2:11).

It would be one thing to leave a child with a grandparent or relative, but Hannah leaves her son with Eli, an old priest, sloppy in the things of God. Being a mom, her actions take my breath away. How could she just walk away?

Because Hannah trusts God and chooses to live in hope.

Leaving Samuel in Shiloh with Eli is a demonstrative act of thankfulness to God. It is heartbreaking to us, but to Hannah the stigma of barrenness has been lifted. She prayed for a son who would always be in the presence of the Lord even if God's presence is in Shiloh—with Eli. Regardless of her sacrifice, God has demonstrated great kindness to Hannah. Nothing can change that. She is forever thankful, yet there is even more to Hannah's story and her thankfulness.
Hannah and Elkanah have five more children together—three more boys and two girls (1 Samuel 2:21). As for Samuel, Hannah visits him every year when she and Elkanah go to Shiloh to worship. She takes a new coat to Samuel every time she visits (1 Samuel 2:19). Can you imagine the joy in her heart as she makes that yearly journey, introducing Samuel to a new sibling year after year, while also marveling at all the Lord is doing in her eldest? Her tender mother's heart must ache with joy.

Perhaps because I am older and sense the days passing quickly, I long for time with my adult children. I relish the deep, mature conversations my adult children offer me. I want to see my grandchildren too! I am thankful for the ministry the Lord has given me, but I often ache for my family. Reflecting on my own desires while also exploring the thankful heart of Hannah, a small, interesting detail about Hannah and Samuel captured my attention.

*"Now Samuel judged Israel all the days of his life. And he used to go annually on circuit to Bethel and Gilgal and Mizpah, and he judged Israel in all these places. **Then his return was to Ramah**, for he had a house there, and there he judged Israel; and there he built an alter to the Lord" (1 Samuel 7:15-17).*

Do you see it? As an adult, Samuel makes Ramah his home. Hannah lives in Ramah. For Samuel's mother, God's blessings have come full circle.

Maybe in her old age she recalls the heartache of childlessness or the ridicule of Peninnah. She remembers, as a young mother, the odd mixture of joy and pain in leaving her first born with Eli. Yet now, as an older woman, she is able to experience the joy of her other five children and perhaps grandchildren. As an aging mother, she looks upon her first-born son, Samuel, understanding he is a powerful leader for God's people, purposed for God's plans. With a thankful heart she can acknowledge, "If I had not been there, I would not be here."

For many of us, life has unfolded differently than we imagined. It has for me. I never imagined being a widow, married again to a widower, blending a family, grieving a prodigal, or battling cancer. Neither did I imagine having a fruitful ministry in Cuba, writing two books, doing life with a second precious husband, or loving five children and five grandchildren. The Lord does not give us the option of re-living our lives. No do-overs. Neither is He obligated to restore all that we lose to sin, sickness, and sorrow. Like Hannah, I can see the goodness of the Lord in all of the heartache and pain. I can be thankful regardless of any circumstance. I can say confidently, because of Christ, "If I had not been there, I would not be here." Like you, I can choose to live in hope.

Thankful praying, and certainly thankful living, is not dependent on happy endings. Most assuredly, Hannah had disappointments and hardships throughout her life. We all do.

But her hope, and ours, is in the confident expectation that God will do what He says He will do. He will keep His promises. He will use all things, even heartache, for His glory and our good. He will never leave us or forsake us. All of God's blessings are ours in Christ even when we cannot see them, feel them, or understand them. We can pray **and** live as thankful people because we are anchored in hope.

As I close this chapter, I am overwhelmed again by the privilege of prayer, knowing that through it, Almighty God allows us to participate in His eternal plans. Oh, may we live daily in our privilege. I am equally overwhelmed that Almighty God desires a relationship with us, deepened and expanded through prayer. He beckons us to the throne of grace and mercy so we may pour out both our smallest and greatest concerns. Prayer does not simply change circumstances, it changes us. Run to prayer, dear one. Pray with hope.

Discussion Questions

Read 1 Samuel 1:1-28

1. "When God wants to change the course of events, He calls out an intercessor." Does this statement alarm you or does it encourage you to pray?

2. What does it mean to pray in Jesus' name?

3. Read Hebrews 4:16. Believers in Christ have been invited to pray. Why then do we often neglect prayer? How does sin affect our prayers?

4. Read Psalm 37:3. There are two phrases or parts to this verse. Discuss how the second phrase is dependent on the first phrase. How does this verse change the way we often view pray?

5. Read Colossians 1:9-12. Based on Paul's prayer for the Colossian Christians, what would you like for the Lord do in your own life, and in the lives of those you love?

5

ANNA
Hope for the Waiting

My fifth grandchild was recently born. The thrill of each birth never gets old. The moment my husband and I get the announcement a new baby is expected until the day that bundle of joy arrives, we embark on an exciting journey of anticipation. We mark the due date on our calendar, we buy baby items, we ponder what the gender will be, and we wonder aloud what our children will name their new addition......and we wait. Certainly our anticipation is riveted with gladness. We know a precious baby is on the way, but like kids waiting for Christmas, it seems the day will never arrive. The wait, however long it may seem, is always worth it.

Anna is a woman who is waiting. She has spent her entire long life anticipating the greatest event in history. Even though her story covers only three verses in Luke, her example conveys a world of truth to all of us. So who is Anna, what is she anticipating, and how does she demonstrate hope? Lean in, dear reader. You are going to love her.

Who is Anna?

Anna is a widow. As a young woman, she was married for only seven years; however, when Luke introduces her, she is eighty-four years old (Luke 2:36-37). While she has been a widow most of her life, it appears Anna has never been idle; neither has she been filled with self-pity. For decades, she has actively served the Lord in the temple in Jerusalem. In fact, Scripture seems to indicate she lives at the temple. Several Old Testament passages describe rooms or living quarters around the perimeter of the temple or on the temple grounds. It is possible Anna lives in one of these rooms.

Luke also gives us a tidbit of her ancestral history. She is from the tribe of Asher, one of the ten apostate tribes of Northern Israel who broke away after the reign of Solomon. These ten tribes instituted a false religion and God eventually judged them using the Assyrians. Because of the cruel tactics of Assyria, an entire new people group called Samaritans emerged from Northern Israel. To the true Jew, Samaritans were loathsome half-breeds. Many from Anna's ancestral tribe would have become Samaritans—but not Anna's family.

Anna is living on the temple grounds and operating freely within the temple. No Samaritan would be allowed to do that. Many historians believe Anna's ancient family migrated south to Jerusalem, forsaking the false religion of the Northern Kingdom before the Assyrian invasion. The tiny tidbit of Anna's ancestry in Luke 2:36 reveals she has faithfulness in her distant past. She has been blessed with a Godly heritage to build upon because her ancient family chose hope for future generations.

Anna is also described as a prophetess, a woman who speaks and teaches the truth of God's Word with spiritual authority. She is not foretelling future events, but she is relying on God's Word to understand future events. Her knowledge of Scripture is reflected in her words and manifested in her actions. She serves...constantly. The phrase "serving night and day" may not be a literal twenty-four hours on her feet, but it speaks of a life given over to serving the Lord by serving other people (Luke 2:37).

Her constant service, however, is not frenzied activity; rather it is service saturated in prayer with fasting. She is a woman of intense prayer who knows the Word of God. Her life is focused God-ward; therefore, her prayers move in the same direction as the heart of God. Eternity alone will reveal all God has accomplished through the prayers and service of Anna.

I love her already. I want to sit at her feet and listen or follow in her footsteps and observe. I want to hear her pray and see God at work around her. Yet there is still more of her story to unpack.

Three times Luke affirms that God's people are waiting with expectancy for God's Messiah (Luke 2:25, 2:38, and 3:16). When Luke writes, Rome is the occupying power. It is an oppressive rule characterized by heavy taxation, burdensome servitude, and cruel authority. It would be normal to desire freedom from such tyranny, but the Jewish longing for God's Messiah is not indulgent or wishful thinking. Their anticipation is based on Old Testament prophesies. While certainly some Jews have given up any hope of a Messiah, Anna has not.

Anna is confident the Word of God stands forever based on the faithful character of God (Isaiah 40:8). She knows God has had a plan for His people from the beginning, and nothing, not even Rome, can thwart those plans (Isaiah 46:9-10). She understands the prophetic writings of Isaiah, Jeremiah, Ezekiel, and Habakkuk, and she sees the work of the Lord unfolding exactly as the prophets foretold. But above all, based on the Old Testament, Anna knows the Messiah is coming.

"But as for you Bethlehem Ephrathah, too little to be among the clans of Judah, from you One will go forth for Me to be ruler in Israel. His goings forth are from long ago, from the days of eternity" (Micah 5:2-4).

"Behold My Servant, whom I uphold; My chosen one in whom My soul delights, I have put my Spirit upon Him; He will bring forth justice to the nations" (Isaiah 42:1).

Anna is well aware of the rich prophecies from the Old Testament concerning God's Messiah, but the writings of Daniel give a time frame for her hope. Daniel 9:24-27 organizes future events in *weeks*. A *week* represents seven years. Daniel writes of *seven weeks* and *sixty-two weeks* in the context of rebuilding the temple destroyed by the Babylonians and the advent of God's Messiah.

Jewish history and Old Testament prophecy were studied extensively in Anna's day. At the time of Luke's writing, the Jewish people knew the exact dates ancient King Cyrus of Persia had sent a group of exiled Jews back to Jerusalem to rebuild the temple (2 Chronicles 36:22-23). According to Daniel, the rebuilding of the temple and the walls of Jerusalem would take seven weeks or forty-nine years. After the temple was completed, there would be a span of 62 weeks or 434 years until the Messiah comes.

Don't miss this! Anna, along with every other knowledgeable Jew, knows she is living near the end of those 434 years. The time has come! Based on God's Word through Daniel's prophecy, Messiah's arrival is imminent! God's people are living in anticipation—waiting with great hope. In light of God's Word, Anna has chosen to adjust her entire life to live in her hope—every single day.

Living in Her Hope

If Anna had a life-verse, it might very well be *"In Thy presence is fullness of joy" (Psalm16:11)*. While Luke writes *she never left the temple*, we would be remiss to believe she lives a sequestered, lonely life within the confines of a building. Anna's life is much more vibrant than that. She sees the Lord in everything she does and in every event around her. Her life is infused with immense vitality and hope. She chooses to surround herself with God's presence whether through prayer, fasting, or service to others. Her daily routine is an outward expression of her inner hope—the Messiah is coming.

It appears Anna has no children or extended family; otherwise, she would live in their care. Living in a borrowed room at the temple, at a typically vulnerable season of life, suggests a simple, frugal, unencumbered life. She is not burdened with the cares of the world; neither does she desire the things of the world. However, she is not an ascetic nor does she live with her head in the sand, oblivious to the oppression of her countrymen. Instead, her laser-focused living is directed toward the greatest hope for her people and indeed the entire world. Her hope is the Christ.

It is difficult for me to imagine such a life, uncluttered by a million tiny details and unrushed by other people's demands. The best example my mind can produce is an East Tennessee woman named Mrs. Iris Edwards. Everyone called her Mrs. E.

Mrs. E. lived a simple life. She and her late husband had worked hard, raised a sweet family, and led by Godly example. She had a calm and quiet way about her. It proved to be a magnet, drawing people to her gentleness. Without saying a word, Mrs. E. radiated Jesus.

Often she would invite my late husband, who was her pastor, to come to her house for breakfast. Dana always agreed. He would sit at her simple kitchen table, which slanted slightly because of the aging floor. He would eat the scrambled eggs she cooked in an iron skillet in her modest kitchen, and he would soak in her love and encouragement. Mrs. E. prayed for her pastor during those early morning breakfast meetings, using God's Word to plant hope into his life. Dana always came home spiritually refreshed after sitting awhile with Mrs. E.

Because our East Tennessee church was experiencing a surge of college students, Dana asked Mrs. E. if she would disciple some of the college-age women. Standing on her front porch, she pondered Dana's question, cocking her head to one side as if she had no understanding of what he meant by *disciple*. He tried to explain.

"You know. Teach them how to walk with the Lord. Teach them how to read the Bible and how to pray."

Again, Mrs. E. looked perplexed. Her thoughtful, yet simple, reply surprised him.

"Dana, how can I teach someone to fall in love?"

To me, Anna looks like Mrs. Iris Edwards. Anna simply loves God. She radiates with that love, and she trusts God will keep His Word. Every morning, Anna rises with an expectation of God's promises coming to fruition—not a hundred years in the future, but that very moment! She gladly ponders if this will be the day Messiah will come. Her work and her waiting overflow with joyful hope.

Finally, the day comes.

Anna's story is masterfully interwoven with the account of another aging believer named Simeon (Luke 2:21-35). Simeon is described as a devout and righteous man. Like Anna, he knows the time is right for the Messiah to come. The Holy Spirit has revealed to Simeon that he will not die until he has seen the Lord's Christ (Luke 2:26).

In accordance to Jewish law, Mary and Joseph bring their infant son, Jesus, to the temple to be circumcised and officially named. Afterwards, the young family will offer a sacrifice, quietly observing all the Law requires. On the same day, Simeon is in the temple and the Bible specifically states, the Holy Spirit is upon him (Luke 2:27). Simeon is keenly aware of God's presence. Certainly, his spiritual eyes are alert and his heart receptive to whatever God reveals.

Without detail or fanfare, Simeon sees the young family and their infant son. Immediately, he knows the child is the Christ. Aging Simeon takes Jesus in his arms and pours out a blessing to God.

"Now Lord, Thou dost let Thy bond-servant depart in peace, according to Thy word; For my eyes have seen Thy salvation which Thou hast prepared in the presence of all peoples, A Light Of Revelation To The Gentiles, and the glory of Thy people , Israel" (Luke 2:29-32).

It is uncertain if Simeon pours out his thanks while quietly huddled in a corner with the bewildered family or if he spreads his arms heavenward, loudly proclaiming his unabashed joy. Regardless of Simeon's volume or posture, Anna walks by at that very moment (Luke 2:38). She too immediately knows. Because her spiritual senses are so finely tuned to look for the Messiah, there is no doubt Simeon is holding in his arms God's eternal plan for the ages. Hope has finally come.

Like Simeon, Anna is filled with thanksgiving. She cannot contain her joy and tells everyone she meets the good news. Every downcast person who encounters this radiant woman will have their world shaken by her joyful news. *Christ has come. Hope is alive. God is a promise-keeping God.*

Living in Our Hope

I travel to Cuba often. For the past ten years, the Lord has graciously blessed me with the opportunity to work with the Cuban church and with Cuban women in particular. My husband, Allen, introduced me to Cuba. He has been ministering there since 1992, and soon after we married, he urged me to go with him. I gladly agreed, never dreaming Cuba would become a major focus of my ministry today.

Like so many American Christians venturing into other countries, I thought I had something to offer the women of Cuba. I thought they needed me. As it turns out, I needed them. I needed their perspective, their earnest thankful prayers, and the sound of their heartfelt worship. I needed to hear their hope. I will never forget the exact moment I realized, like Anna the prophetess, Cuban Christians are yearning for Christ to come again—not a hundred years from now, but today!

Truthfully, in that moment of realization, I couldn't remember the last time I yearned for the coming Messiah. I had become like the Israelites of old, satisfied and on the verge of complacency (Deuteronomy 6:10-12). Certainly, there is a difference between contentment and complacency. Meeting Christian Cuban women who were content, yet still filled with hopeful anticipation, led me to understand I needed a fresh perspective of Christ' return.

In Scripture, Jesus speaks often about His second coming. He warns us of the turbulence that will precede His coming: wars and rumors of wars, hatred, betrayal, falling away from faith, and false prophets preaching lies (Matthew24:6-12). He emphasizes the quickness of His second coming, urging us to prepare today and wait with anticipation (Matthew 25:1-13). But Jesus also breathes words of comfort, soothing any fears we might have about His return.

"Let not your hearts be troubled; believe in God, believe also in Me. In My Father's house are many dwelling places; if it

*were not so, I would have told you; for I go to prepare a place for you. And if I go and prepare a place for you, **I will come again** and receive you to Myself; that where I am, there you may be also" (John 14:1-3).*

All of us need our focus readjusted from time to time. It's easy to get caught up in the busyness of life. Jobs, families, responsibilities, and relationships take a lot of time and energy, which can easily overshadow any thought of a returning Messiah. So how then do we live in the tension of being all in, here and now, while also waiting with expectancy for Christ to return? To do both seems like walking with one foot on the street and one on the curb. We may be making progress, but it is slow and off balanced at best. Certainly God doesn't expect us to be like the dozens of groups throughout history who have neglected the present to sit on a hill and wait for the Messiah's return. Then, how on earth do we live each day in the hope of Jesus' second coming?

The answer lies in two practical truths. First, we must get a fresh perspective of who Christ is and how He will return. Second, we must live unencumbered lives as we wait.

Fresh Perspective

The Apostle John was probably the youngest of the twelve disciples. He outlived all the other disciples, and history indicates he was the only one not martyred. Yet his long and fruitful life was not free of turmoil and heartache. In his later years, John was exiled to the island of Patmos, conscripted to hard labor for his outspoken Christian leadership in Ephesus. While on Patmos, the Holy Spirit gave John a vision, a revelation of Christ. His written record is the book of Revelation, a divinely inspired account of Jesus' second coming and the final book of the New Testament.

John's record of the revelation of Christ is not intended

to produce fear in believers. Its goal is hope. John reminds us the return of Christ is imminent (Revelation 1:3). In light of that truth, we are to prepare for it and anticipate it with great hope. The return of Christ is not a faraway event without any bearing on the here and now. In fact, the opposite is true. It should influence and shape every detail of our lives.

John's vision of Jesus in the first chapter jars me every time I read it (Revelation 1:9-16). It seems I have become accustomed to a gentler, meeker Jesus than the one pictured in Revelation. C.S. Lewis addresses this common misconception in his children's series *The Chronicles of Narnia.* Two memorable characters, Susan and Mr. Beaver, are having a conversation about Aslan, the great representative Lion.

"Aslan is a lion-The Lion, the great Lion."
"Ooh," said Susan. "I'd thought he was a man. Is he quite safe? I shall feel rather nervous about meeting a lion."
"Safe?" said Mr. Beaver. "Who said anything about safe? 'Course he isn't safe. But he's good. He's the King, I tell you."
(C.S. Lewis, *The Lion, the Witch, and the Wardrobe*)

John's vision of Jesus is not safe; instead—it inspires awe. Read it with fresh eyes.

"I turned to see whose voice it was that spoke to me. When I turned I saw seven golden lampstands, and among the lampstands was One like the Son of Man, dressed in a long robe, and with a gold sash wrapped around His chest. His head and His hair were white like wool—white as snow—and His eyes like a fiery flame. His feet were like bronze as it is fired in a furnace, and His voice like the sound of cascading waters. He had seven stars in His right hand; a sharp double-edged sword came from His mouth, and His face was shining like the sun at midday" (Revelation 1:12-16 HCSB).

The appearance of Jesus in John's vision is vastly different from the Jesus of Nazareth who changed John's life forever. He remembers the voice and appearance of Jesus. For three years, he walked with Jesus, listened to Him teach, and watched Him work miracles. John also experienced the authority of Jesus as He cleansed the temple and confronted the Pharisees. John saw Jesus crucified and then beheld Him after the resurrection. But John has never, never seen anything like the glorified Christ. His response is both awe and worship, *"And when I saw Him, I fell at His feet as a dead man"* (Revelation 1:17).

Jesus is no longer the sweet baby in a manger. He is not the gentle teacher on a hillside. Neither is He the dying figure on a cruel cross. Instead, He is the risen, glorified Christ of all eternity. His attire defines Him as our high priest, the Ancient of Days, the Righteous Judge, and the conquering King. This is Jesus Christ, revealed in all of God's glory and no one—not Moses or Ezekiel or Saul of Tarsus on the road to Damascus and not even John the beloved disciple—can behold Him. This Jesus does not bring goosebumps and warm fuzzies. Instead, He commands awe and wonder and worship.

And yet John writes, *"He laid His right hand upon me, saying, "Do not be afraid..."* (Revelation 1:17b). Jesus says the same thing to us as we anticipate His coming again. *"Do not be afraid, dear believer, I AM the First and the Last—the most important in time, place, and order who will bring about the completion of all things. Don't be afraid of living, dear child of God; I hold the keys to life. And don't be afraid of dying either; I hold the keys to death as well"* (Revelation 1:17-18 paraphrased). Do you see it? Fear is not the objective. Awe wrapped in love is.

John's magnificent vision of the Messiah is *our* Jesus. This is who Christ is today, and this is who will return. Refresh your mind's image of Him and be inspired with new hope. He will come quickly. He will set all things right. Our present sufferings will pale in light of His coming (Romans 8:18). Rest assured He is not coming to condemn His children but to gather us to Himself. He loves us. He has redeemed us. He is coming for us. Yes, we are to be filled with awe and worship but our response is equally one of love and thankfulness—ongoing to see His face.

When I was a child, my father sometimes traveled out of town or out of the country. While our family missed him, my brother, and sister, and I knew he would return—with presents! Oh, we eagerly waited for him to walk through the door, bearing gifts for his children. But our mom waited with different motivation. Of course, he always brought her a gift too, but the gift was not what drew her into hopeful waiting. My mom just wanted to see his face and be in his presence. Far exceeding any gifts, she simply loved my daddy and longed to be with him.

Christ will indeed return. Yes, He will bring with Him the ultimate fulfillment of all things, making everything new and all things right. He is the glorified awesome Christ. But do our hearts long for His return simply because we love Him and yearn to be in His presence? Do our souls need a fresh adjustment as we anticipate His coming? He is the coming King and also the loving groom coming for His bride. Will you wait with longing? Will you live expectantly with hope? Are you willing to adjust your life in preparation of His return?

Unencumbered Living

The Jewish temple in Anna's day is not a quiet cathedral. It is a busy place filled with all kinds of people. Anna never leaves the temple because there is plenty of work to do there and hundreds of people who need her ministry. She does not sequester herself in an isolated closet void of human interaction. She serves—people—in the temple. Her service to others is undergirded by a devoted life of prayer. She is in constant communion with the Lord even while serving the people around her.

You and I do not live in a temple made of stone. We *are* the temple! The Holy Spirit of Christ indwells us—living in us permanently (2 Corinthians 6:16). Unlike Anna who constantly served the Lord on the physical grounds of the temple, we take the temple with us everywhere we go. Everything we do, everything we say, every thought we think, and every prayer we pray emanates from within us—the temple of God. Reading Psalm 29:9 with New Testament eyes is sobering, *"And in His temple everything says, 'Glory!'"*

Does it? If we are the temple, does everything about our lives give honor to God? Does everything say "Glory"?

Of course, I am not writing about some kind of sinless perfection. I am, however, urging each of us to allow the Holy Spirit to examine our lives, to shine the spotlight of His Word into the deepest recesses of our souls, and expose what needs to be swept out of our personal temple. Anna experiences great freedom and joy because she lives an unencumbered life—*a life swept clean of sin, the disappointments of the past, and the cares of the world.* We have this same hope! But how?

Freedom from sin. Sin can be the greatest deterrent of hope in the life of a believer. It seems like an obvious point, yet many Christians wonder why they feel weighed down, hopeless, lacking joy and peace. Many times, sin is the culprit. It creates bondage, guilt, and condemnation. Left unchecked and unconfessed, sin entangles us, choking out the freedom Christ longs to give.

Jesus said, *"You shall know the truth and the truth shall make you free"* (John 8:32). We have slapped that verse across everything from civil rights to comedy routines, but Jesus is speaking of Himself and the salvation He offers by grace. He follows up that powerful, but often misquoted verse, with, *"If, therefore, the Son shall make you free, you shall be free indeed"* (John 8:36). Salvation through Christ sets us free from the eternal penalty of sin, but He also sets us free from the power of sin in our daily lives. Like hope, however, we must choose to live in our freedom.

Anna chooses to live each day in the presence of God. Her relationship with Him is up to date. If anything is amiss in her thoughts, attitude, or actions, she readily brings it to the Lord in prayer. Scripture indicates she is in constant communion with God. Her spiritual senses are alert to His Word and His direction. Her unrestrained life of service to the Lord is proof that sin has not been left to fester and infect her life. She chooses peace and joy by keeping the slate clean—everyday.

"If we confess our sin, He is faithful and just to forgive us our sins and cleanse us from all unrighteousness" (1 John 1:9). Confession is an uncomplicated process if we make it a daily, and sometimes an immediate, response to sin. When we confess our sin, we are not giving the Lord new information or surprising Him with our misdeeds. We are simply agreeing with Him about what He already knows. Confession frees us to receive the forgiveness and cleansing that has been there all along.

God desires freedom from the suffocating effects of sin in the lives of His children. He does not want us to grovel in guilt or condemnation. He will never hang yesterday's confessed sin over our heads today. Neither does He want us to live haphazard or sloppy lives, becoming insensitive to sin. He uses the Holy Spirt within us and the Word of God to spotlight anything which needs to be confessed and forsaken. Spending time daily with the Lord, in His Word and in prayer, is not a dusty duty. It is an opportunity to quietly surrender ourselves anew each day, allowing the Lord to adjust, expose, or expel anything that hinders freedom. Confession is an expression of a tender, surrendered life. Oddly, surrender to Christ is the greatest place of freedom.

Freedom from sin makes an obvious difference in

our daily living. When sin is not weighing us down, we are free to love and serve others. Most assuredly, we are free to experience peace and joy in the process. The daily practice of dealing with sin guards us from living in fear. It keeps us from looking over our shoulder to see if we will be caught. It brings an inner peace that permeates every relationship and situation. Freedom from sin is not simply looking at life through rose-colored glasses; rather it is experiencing the unhindered work of the Holy Spirit within us.

Freedom from the past. It is safe to assume there are hurts in Anna's past. Like every young bride, she married with the hope of a long and blissful marriage, presumably blessed with children, and perhaps someday grandchildren. Life, however, does not work out this way for Anna. She is widowed after seven short years, leaving her with no children and little assurances about the future. There is no fault or blame to assign for her circumstances, just difficult days that can be either her undoing or her uplifting.

So much of life depends on what we do with our past.

I recently read a quote by an unknown author which grabbed my attention. *"If you don't heal what hurt you, you'll bleed on people who didn't cut you."* While there is profound truth in that statement, there is a greater truth for believers in Christ. We cannot heal ourselves. Only Christ can sufficiently heal the hurts of the past, and He is longing to do it. His healing is wrapped in great love, expressed to us through grace and mercy. He does not erase the past, dear friend, but He redeems it, making something beautiful and God-honoring out of our sorrow and brokenness.

If we live long enough, all of us will have a past littered with some degree of baggage, sin, grief, or hurt. No one is exempt, and none of us has the right or responsibility to cast judgement on someone else's past. As you read the next few

110

pages, I want you to sit still and soak in the goodness of the Lord. I want you to understand the depths of His grace. I am praying as you read, you will embrace the freedom He longs to give.

"Forgetting what lies behind and reaching forward to what lies ahead, I press on..." (Philippians 3:13b-14a). The Bible is not suggesting a flippant dismissal of the past. Neither is the Apostle Paul relying on some kind of mysterious amnesia to erase the past. He is, however, saying the past does not have to control the future. Throughout Scripture, over and over, person after person, one message resounds loudly. God's grace is sufficient to cover the past. Anyone's past. Even yours. Even mine.

Our wounds can come from a multitude of sources including our own sin, someone else's sin against us, or simply the difficulties of life. Grace, however, allows us to view the past through a different lens. Certainly, we cannot change the past, but by the grace of God we can view it with hope. I have emphasized Isaiah 43:18-19 throughout this book. It speaks volumes to the dilemma of our past. Read it again—out loud.

"Do not call to mind the former things, or ponder things of the past. Behold I will do something new, now it will spring forth; will you not be aware of it? I will even make a roadway in the wilderness, rivers in the desert."

Like Paul, the writer is not telling us to forget the past. He is saying, however, don't get stuck there. Stop rehearsing the wounds and then sitting in the dust of despair. Instead, look forward—with hope. God is doing a new thing in your life. By grace, He is making something new in the wilderness that has permeated your life thus far. He is pouring out rivers of purpose on the parched places of your past. This is not Pollyanna jargon. It is truth based on the unfailing, faithful character of God. But precious reader, *you must choose to live in truth.*

111

Walk slowly with me through some difficult principles about hope and freedom as it pertains to our past.

Certainly, some of us are living with ongoing consequences of personal sin from our past—sin we have confessed and forsaken, yet it still has an effect on us today. Living in freedom from a sinful past requires acceptance of the forgiveness God offers. Our acceptance of God's forgiveness has nothing to do with feelings. It has everything to do with faith. Faith is not only believing God but also acting on what we believe. In faith, we accept His forgiveness, and we live like a forgiven person, empowered by the Holy Spirit to move forward into whatever plans God has for our future. Faith is also demonstrated by verbally expressing thanks for His forgiveness even when we cannot understand it, feel it, or see the immediate effects of it. Faith moves us away from our sinful past and towards the unearned, unmerited grace of God.

God's grace knows no limits. It supersedes any sin, any shortcoming, or any shortsighted decision in our past. The wonder of His grace is conveyed in Romans 8:28, *"And we know that all things work together for good to those who love God...."* He uses even the consequences of sin to work for His glory and our good. Only grace can do that. So often I am humbled to recall how the Lord saved me at a young age, knowing full well my most grievous sins were ahead of me. He loved me anyway. He saved me anyway. He forgave me anyway. Even now, I am typing through tears, knowing He has used the sinful choices of yesterday to bring me to this moment. Only God's grace can do that. He can do the same for you.

Recently, I met a remarkable woman in Cuba. I had been leading a conference for women, teaching about grace. Afterwards she shared with me her story. It began rather humorously.

"*All my teeth are false,*" she abruptly stated, and clicked a full set of dentures out of her mouth to show me. I smiled, trying to disguise my surprise.

"*I have scars everywhere,*" she continued, lifting up the hem of her skirt just a little, to expose legs resembling a Rand McNally road map.

I was now genuinely curious, so I pulled her aside; listening intently to what I sensed would be a riveting story.

Years ago I was in a terrible car accident. The driver and my best friend were killed. I was thrown from the car. All my teeth were knocked out. Many bones in my face were broken. My entire body was so cut and mangled—no one thought I would live. But I did.

She looked at the floor, as she continued.

When I got out of the hospital, I was so ugly; I thought no man would ever love me. I was just a college student and I didn't know the Lord. I became involved with one of my professors. He took advantage of my youth and my despair. I knew our affair was wrong, but I thought he loved me—until I became pregnant. He left me and never acknowledged the son I gave birth to.

After a few quiet moments, that dear woman's eyes finally brightened and she finished her story.

Years later I heard the good news of Christ. I received God's forgiveness and His salvation. I married a wonderful Christian man. We began serving in our church. My husband loved my little son but we wanted children together, raising all of them in a Godly home. Instead, I had four miscarriages. We were never able to have children.

113

I have often wondered why God would allow my only surviving child to be the one born out of a sinful affair. Today, I think I know.

My son is a grown man now. He loves the Lord and serves in his church. When I look at my only son, born out of sin—all I see is grace. I can't claim anything but grace—not a godly marriage, not a life of service, not an ounce of righteousness— just grace. My one precious son is a reminder that my past is covered with grace.

Grace changes the way we view the past. God does not erase the past—but by grace, He redeems it. Whatever sin has left you scarred, Christ can make all things new. He is making roadways in the wilderness and rivers in the desert—simply by grace. This is our hope, and we must choose to live in it.

Unfortunately, some of us have debris in our past put there by someone else. Someone else hurt us or abused us or disappointed us. Someone else's sin created the scar on our soul, and maybe it was someone who was supposed to love and care for us. Regardless of who hurt us or how deep the wound or how far reaching the consequences, it is never God's desire for us to be shackled and defeated by the past. His desire is for each of us to live an unencumbered life—a life of freedom— even freedom from the past, no matter how dark or horrific it may be.

The solution is forgiveness.

Forgiveness is not dismissal of the pain or denial of the consequences. It is not letting the perpetrator off the hook; neither is it inviting that person back into your life. Biblical forgiveness is releasing. It is releasing your hurt and anger to the Lord, trusting Him to heal the wounds in your heart. Forgiveness is also releasing the guilty person to the Lord, allowing God to either take His vengeance or restore a life with grace. You and I cannot remove sin from someone's life, but we can release the person from shame and any debt that person may owe us. In doing so, we release ourselves from inner destruction.

Forgiveness is a difficult and often misunderstood principle. It is not a "get over it" mentality, and usually, it is not a one-time event. But when we are willing to practice Biblical forgiveness, we are allowing the Lord to redeem the ashes of the past. I did not say He restores everything we have lost or all that has been stolen from us. But He redeems—buying back our sorrows and transforming them into something of great value.

Forgiving others requires our surrender to Christ. It is a demonstration of trust in the One who is well acquainted with our pain, our hurt, and our disappointments. Forgiving the one who wounded us is an acknowledgment that Christ alone is our healer and He is faithful to His Word. When we offer Biblical forgiveness, we are *choosing to live in hope.* Certainly, forgiveness does not supply us with easy answers to the difficult question, *"Why?"* It will, however, clear the path for God's redeeming, healing work—His roadway into the wilderness.

Years ago, God brought a wonderful Christian woman into my life to help me through a particularly difficult season. If you met my friend Judy, you would think she had led a charmed life. She was perky and smiley, a minister's wife, and a snazzy dresser. Her past, however, was anything but charmed.

Judy grew up on the east side of Saint Louis. Both of her parents were alcoholics. She watched them divorce and remarry multiple times before her mother finally moved Judy and her siblings to another state when Judy was in high school. But while growing up in St. Louis, Judy and her siblings experienced violent cruelty from her father. He often came home in a drunken rage, physically beating anyone who got in his way, including Judy, who was the youngest. Her older brothers tried to protect her, taking the beatings in hopes their dad would pass out before he got to Judy. Sometimes it worked.

Even while growing up in such atrocities, my precious friend was invited to church. As a child, she heard the gospel and surrendered her life to Christ. But her father's abuse did not stop. In fact, it intensified. She recalls the owner of the bar where her mother worked putting her on a city bus and telling her to stay on it all day so her drunken raging father could not find her. Eventually, she had to return home. Mercy was not waiting.

When Judy's mother finally left and relocated the family, there was a semblance of peace. My friend graduated from high school, attended a Christian Bible college, met and married a young man in ministry, and eventually the happy couple had a precious little girl. It seemed Judy was moving forward with her life and indeed the past was in the past—until she accepted an invitation to a family gathering back in St. Louis.

Her father showed up at the reunion, and miraculously, he wasn't drunk. He was even cordial, scooping up his granddaughter, Judy's little girl, into his arms. At the sight of her father holding her daughter, something inside my friend snapped. A tsunami of fear, anxiety, and hate overtook her, and she couldn't shake it even after she returned home.

Her emotional state quickly turned inward, and Judy began to experience turmoil in the very things that once brought great joy. She finally confided in an older Godly woman in her church. This wise and tender woman listened carefully and then asked a startling question, *"Judy, have you ever forgiven your father?"* Judy had never considered it, but she was willing to be obedient to whatever the Lord asked of her. Privately, she asked God to change her heart towards her dad. A few years later, the Lord gave her an opportunity to confront her father.

A telephone call came. Judy's dad was in the hospital, dying from liver failure due to alcoholism. The family wanted her to be there. She agreed to travel back to St. Louis and see her father for the last time.

Years after the fact, Judy and I sat in her living room, calmly drinking coffee while she told me of that final meeting with her dad.

When I walked into his room, no one else was there. The lights were dim, and the only sound was the clicking of monitors and machines around my father. His skin was yellow from liver failure, and he was barely conscious. I sat down in the chair beside his bed and leaned towards him, hoping he could hear me.

"Daddy, you are a wicked man. I remember everything you ever did to me."

His eyes opened, and then widened with understanding. He couldn't speak because of the tubes in his throat, so I continued.

"Daddy, I know what kind of man you are, and God knows too. He even knows things about you that I don't. But, daddy....."

My sweet friend paused her story and smiled at me, "Jennifer, I said to my father the three most powerful words ever spoken. Do you know what they are?"

I shook my head no, even though I assumed those three powerful words were *I love you.*

Judy smiled again and continued her story.

"But, Daddy—I forgive you."

Yellow-jaundiced tears began to stream down my father's face. He reached for my hand and I took his. And then I told him of the forgiveness of Christ and the hope of the gospel. I asked him if he wanted salvation. He squeezed my hand and gave a slight nod. I prayed with him and for him. His tears never ceased to flow, and a supernatural peace settled over the entire room.

My daddy died the next day, but I am absolutely confident I will see him again in heaven—healed and whole. Forgiveness didn't just save my daddy—it saved me too.

Oh, dear reader, do you hear the hope in those powerful three words? Are you willing to live in the freedom they bring? Will you choose a life unencumbered by the past? Please understand. There is great mercy in these paragraphs about forgiveness, and while I am not a counselor or a therapist, I am confident God's Word is true. Hope is real and freedom is possible for all of us. I have wrestled with my own issues of forgiveness and emotional healing, and I have found my Savior to be faithful in doing a good work in me (Philippians 1:6). He will be faithful to you too. No matter how deep the pit or how brutal the scars, He promises to make a roadway in the wilderness and a river in the desert. This is our hope. This is our Jesus.

Freedom from the cares of the world. Anna lives an unencumbered life. She is forward facing, anticipating her coming Messiah. Her joyful service and surrendered life indicate freedom from any crippling sin as well as freedom from the disappointments of the past. However, there is one final observation about Anna. She lives unencumbered by the cares of this world. Somehow, Anna lives above the fray and clutter of this life. She is not entangled in anything that distracts her from her hope, yet she is invested in the lives of others. It sounds impossible, but there are two interwoven qualities that keep Anna moving in the right direction—her contentment and her focus.

Anna lives in a borrowed room. She doesn't have many personal possessions. Her needs are met, but there are few if any luxuries adorning the life she has chosen—and she is content. Contrary to popular belief, her simple life supports and enhances her contentment.

Contentment is an inside job that has nothing to do with what we own. King Solomon was a wealthy king, and yet his heart's cry in Ecclesiastes is *"Vanity, vanity, all is vanity."* He also expressed great wisdom in Proverbs 10:22, *"It is the blessing of the Lord that makes rich, and He adds no sorrow to it."* Solomon understood from firsthand experience there is often sorrow in wealth. But Solomon was wise enough to know that even the quest for wealth can be distracting and unfulfilling. He is not aiming his words to those who have abundance; rather he is aiming his words at every heart who wants to experience contentment. The blessing of the Lord is the greatest wealth anyone can desire because there is no sorrow, no distraction, and no burden in it. Solomon is speaking to both the rich and the poor. The quest for earthy things will never satisfy the soul.

Jesus understands the pressure we feel to take care of families, pay bills, and meet responsibilities, but in the Sermon on the Mount, he addresses the underlying anxiety that often accompanies our daily routine. He wants to calm the frenzied living so many of us default to by adjusting our focus toward a loving Heavenly Father who not only knows our needs but also provides for our needs (Matthew 6:25-34).

Our contentment is a reflection of our trust in God. When we are trusting God, we loosen our grip on the cares of this world. We are confident God will supply every need. Honestly, I have a long way to go in this area. It seems I automatically default to fear, anxiety, and stress when life gets hectic or out of my control. Thankfully, the Lord is long on patience, full of grace and mercy in the complicated fray of life. Soak in His promises:

"...casting all your anxiety upon Him, because He cares for you" (1 Peter 5:7).

"Be anxious for nothing, but in everything by prayer and supplication with thanksgiving, let your requests be made know to God. And the peace of God, which surpasses all comprehension, shall guard your hearts and your minds in Christ Jesus" (Philippians 4:6-7).

"Look at the birds of the air...your Heavenly Father feeds them. Are you not worth much more than they? And which of you can, by being anxious can add a single cubit to your life's span? Seek first His kingdom and His righteousness; and all these things shall be added to you" (Matthew 6:26, 27, & 33). "Be strong, and let your heart take courage, all you who hope in the Lord" (Psalm 31:24).

Anna is content even in the simplicity of her life. She is peaceful on the inside because her trust is focused in the right direction. Her eyes are locked on God, who is her hope. Paul writes, *"Set your mind on things above, not on things that are on earth"* (Colossians 3:17). Interestingly, God does not force us to set our minds, our thoughts, or our focus on things above. It is a choice we make each day as we surrender ourselves to Christ, empowered by His Holy Spirit. *A mind set on things above* certainly does not remove the responsibilities of our earthly life. Instead, it is the motivation and the energy to fulfill those responsibilities for the glory of Christ—while we wait for His return.

Conclusion

Three verses from Luke's gospel have generated the longest chapter in *Women of Hope*. Anna is the only woman of the seven presented in this book who, from the moment we meet her, has no crisis of hope. She has weathered enough years to understand her hope is in the faithful promises of God. Her soul is firmly anchored, and because of it, she is living in great freedom. Her simple life is fully focused on her Lord, unencumbered by the entanglement of sin, the disappointments of the past, or the cares of this world. With spiritual clarity and earthly purpose, she anticipates her Messiah's coming.

Oh, to follow her example.

Ponder for a few moments the second coming of Christ. Are you longing to see His face? Are you living each day with hope-filled anticipation? Are you experiencing freedom while you wait—freedom from sin, freedom from the past, freedom from the cares of this world? Will you allow the Lord to release you from anything keeping you in bondage? I understand there are sins, wounds, and cares so deep and so wide freedom seems impossible. Certainly, simple answers do not negate complicated circumstances. Yet I am confident— the Lord will supply every need in order for us to live in hope. The question remains. Will you choose to live in your hope—while you wait for Christ' return?

Discussion Questions

Read Luke 2:36-38

1. Is there anything about Anna or this chapter that particularly resonates with you?

2. How do we live in the tension of being all in, here and now, while also waiting with expectancy for Christ to return?

3. Does John's vision of Jesus in Revelation 1:12-16 comfort you or does it alarm you? Does it change the way you envision Christ?

4. "So much of life depends on what we do with the past." How does the Lord deal with our past? How does forgiveness free us to move forward?

5. What is the difference between contentment and complacency? Read Philippians 4:11-13. How can we learn to be content?

6

MARTHA
Hope for Every Personality

A blended family has challenges. That may be the
greatest understatement ever written. When my husband Allen
and I put our two families together, we had no idea what to
expect. Neither of us had any experience with blended families.
We were honestly naïve, and maybe a little foolish, in our
assumption that everyone would get along and we could be the
new millennium Brady Bunch. Oh my! Were we wrong!

    In the early years of our marriage, there were days I
could not even leave the room without a fight breaking out
among the children. A real fight. Fists flying, people yelling,
things broken. The older three children left home as quickly
as possible, while the younger two duked it out for a couple
of years before deciding to, at least, be friends. As a family,

we were a mess. Even as a married couple, we had so much to learn about each other.

It seems all seven of us approach life differently—both then and now. I am a Southerner. Lots of "bless her heart" and "yes, ma'am" and "oh, I'm fine." I *feel* everything and tend to overthink to the point of exhaustion. I married, however, a man from the Mid-West—a no-nonsense, bottom line, born leader, and a man of action who seldom allows any grass to grow under his feet. My children are more like me. His children are more like him. I spent a lot of time in tears during those first years of marriage. Even today, my two biological sons are creatives, almost exclusively right brained in their approach to life. Allen's biological children are more logical and analytical—more left brained in their approach to life. Throw into the mix the differences in gender and birth order, as well as the effects of trauma, and all together we were a recipe for disaster. Thankfully somehow, after 12 years, we are now a family.

For decades, I have enjoyed the writing of Tim LaHaye and his research into the different temperaments and personalities of people (*The Spirit Controlled Temperament*). Writer and speaker, Florence Littauer, takes an insightful and humorous approach to the same subject in her book *Personality Plus*. Both authors have helped me better understand my beautiful, blended family and embrace the truth that each of us has been uniquely created by God. Interestingly, a genre of comic book characters has helped as well.

My sons grew up loving Marvel Comics, especially the X-Men. At first, I didn't quite understand the whole X-Men idea. It seemed that each character was both a good guy *and* a bad guy. They would do something incredibly heroic and then something equally selfish—all in the same episode. I asked my older son about this seeming dilemma. "Mom, they are like real people! Conflicted and complicated." Wow, who knew a twelve-year-old could be so intuitive?

Like my family (and the X-Men), Scripture is filled with interesting people. Sometimes, however, we view Biblical characters as one-dimensional, boring individuals. We want to categorize them as either "good guys" or "bad guys" instead of seeing them as unique and colorful— filled with flaws, shortcomings, intelligence, and personality. We tend to force them into tight, easy-to-understand, monochromatic boxes instead of applying a little sanctified imagination and viewing them as the complicated and sometimes conflicted people they really are.

In particular, two women in Scripture—sisters—are often falsely labeled as the good sister and the bad sister. Maybe we don't label them intentionally as such, but the implication seems to be there. Mary and Martha appear three times in Scripture, always appearing together. Scores of sermons and messages have evolved from the New Testament accounts of these sisters. Usually Mary comes out smelling like a rose while poor Martha takes yet another tongue lashing. A closer look, however, may give us new perspective—at least about Martha. She is fearfully and wonderfully created. She also has a lot to tell us about hope.

Who is Martha?

Jesus is traveling from town to town, preaching and ministering. His twelve disciples and probably a small group of women and other followers are traveling with Him (Luke 8:1-3). They approach the small village of Bethany just two miles east of Jerusalem, obviously needing a place to rest or at least needing a meal to eat. A woman named Martha greets them and graciously invites Jesus and his fellow travelers into her home (Luke10:38). We have no evidence she has previously met Jesus, but based on her interaction with Him in Luke 10, it is probable she and her siblings have been His friends for some time.

126

Already we know several things about Martha. The Bible says she welcomed Jesus into her home. It was *her* home. It is reasonable to assume she is either widowed or has never been married because no spouse is ever mentioned. The house belongs to her and she welcomes Jesus into it. But remember, Jesus is not traveling alone. He has an entourage of people—at least twelve and possibly more. When Martha opens her home to Jesus, she is inviting a crowd to dinner—and she does it graciously.

Martha is an excellent hostess, welcoming this large group of people, knowing full well it will mean a boatload of work for her. Since the home is hers, she is responsible for managing it. She has to oversee the preparations, the serving, and the details of feeding and hosting this large group. It will be a labor intensive endeavor, but she welcomes them with open arms. Her attitude says so much about her personality. She is industrious, kindhearted, and a born leader. She gets things done. I am certain she has already formulated a menu, organized her two siblings, and made seating assignments before Jesus ever steps foot inside her door.

All of us need a Martha in our lives. They are practical servants. They get things done in a timely manner. A Martha is not afraid of leadership, difficult projects, or heavy workloads. They are usually direct in their approach to people, but their heart is in the right place. Their efforts are rooted in love. Whether it is in the home, the workplace, or church, we all enjoy the fruit of their labor yet rarely notice who did the work.

My mother is a Martha. She is oldest of eight children, six of them boys. Even today, those six brothers almost salute when my mom walks into the room. She is a born leader, not just because she is the oldest of eight children but because God gifted her with managerial and leadership gifts. She can organize and lead a herd of feral cats—and do it with a smile on her face and a song in her heart—simply because that's the way God wired her. She is a Martha through and through, and our family is blessed because of it.

Through the years, God has blessed me with other women like my mother who lovingly pick up the mantle of Martha and serve. When I first began teaching at my home church in Venice, Florida, the church secretary handed me a sheet of paper organized with lines and grids for information. She asked that I get everyone who attended my Bible study registered with all the appropriate information required on her form. I gladly agreed. Unfortunately, after that first study, she came to collect the infamous sheet of paper. Not one name was on it. I had completely forgotten about that important task the moment she walked out of the room. My mind was on teaching—not collecting registration information. For weeks, the secretary tried to train me and remind me—to no avail. Finally, she put a Martha on the task. Immediately, we had organized registration information suitable for computerized data entry. I was free to concentrate on teaching because a Martha stepped up to the plate and exercised her giftedness. Whew! Thank you, Lord, for Martha!

Jesus accepts the hospitable invitation of Martha. Immediately, we learn she has a sister named Mary who is a study in contrast to practical Martha. Mary is pensive and emotionally expressive, whereas Martha is active and verbally expressive. Mary is tender and maybe easier to get along with than her sister, but remember—Mary does not have to shoulder the responsibility of the household. After all, it isn't her house.

I understand Mary. It isn't that she is more spiritual or better than Martha, she is just wired differently. Her approach to life in general is different than her sister's—like the Speer kids and the Mathewson kids—not better, just different. *In truth, a Mary cannot be a Mary without a Martha somewhere in her life.* Somebody has to do all the things a Mary either doesn't see or has no idea how to accomplish.

As Luke's narrative continues, the differences between these two sisters are on a fast track collision course, and because Mary is probably oblivious to the problem, most of the blame rests on Martha. She loses her perspective in her zeal to serve and, as a result, becomes irritated with her sister—and with Jesus. Her good qualities momentarily get overshadowed by her shortcomings. Perfection usurps excellence and everyone suffers because of it.

The Bible says Mary is sitting at the feet of Jesus, listening to every word He is saying, probably nodding her head in agreement while soaking up His presence until her soul is about to burst. Martha is about to burst too—but not with tender mercy. She is irritated that Mary is not helping with the preparation of food and the serving of guests. In doing the bulk of the work, Martha has gotten overwhelmed with the details, working herself into a frenzy. She lets Jesus know about it (Luke 8:39). In fact, she accuses Jesus of not caring and demands He tell Mary to get up and get busy. To her credit, Martha wants everything to be perfect because she cares deeply about her guests. Unfortunately, perfection is always an elusive pursuit.

A well-meaning perfectionist can easily become critical of others, setting her standards unattainably high. In addition, she can also become critical of herself, shouldering too much responsibility with excessive expectations. A perfectionist tends to lean towards control. Though she wants help, she will not delegate for fear no one can do the job as well as she can. She would rather do things herself—and do it right—and do it her way. Even if someone volunteers to assist her, a Martha tends to micromanage their efforts. She can easily get lost in the details of her task, losing sight of the bigger picture and the real purpose. She is so intent on accomplishing her goal, the perfectionist can become unkind to the people around her.

In Luke 10, Martha gets distracted. She loses sight of her original intent to provide gracious hospitality. Instead, she becomes overwhelmed, doing too many things her way, and eventually becomes critical of both Jesus and her sister. In losing her focus, she also loses her peace and joy. Jesus has to adjust her (Luke 10: 41-42).

Jesus is not condemning her personality. He is adjusting her focus. He gently reminds her to remain attuned to the basic need for food and avoid the pit falls of overachieving perfectionism. Be careful at this point. Every personality type has a unique way of losing focus. Martha is not the bad sister or the less spiritual sister. She is simply more demonstrative, and because of it, her weaknesses are more demonstrative as well.

The second time we meet Martha and Mary in Scripture, tragedy has invaded their lives. Their brother Lazarus has died (John 11: 1-46). Often, when reading this passage, we are so focused on the resurrection of Lazarus we miss the nuances of personalities in play. Again, Martha and Mary are a study in contrast.

The sisters send for Jesus long before Lazarus dies. They fully expect Him to come running, confident Jesus can heal their brother. They both should be commended for their faith. However, instead of coming to Bethany immediately, Jesus tarries two days longer. Jesus' delay is not rejection or dismissal of their request. It is divine timing which will demonstrate the glory of God. In the delay, however, Lazarus dies. While Mary and Martha are overcome with grief, they are also perplexed and disappointed by Jesus' delay. Unsurprisingly, it is Martha who voices her opinion first when Jesus finally arrives—four days after her brother has died (John 11:21).

It is interesting that no one goes with Martha to meet Jesus. A group of Jews have gathered in her home, consoling the sisters after the death of Lazarus, but they all stay put when Martha leaves the house. Later, when Mary goes out to go meet Jesus, all those Jews go with her (John 11:31, 33, 45). This says something about the two women.

Martha does not need anyone to go with her. She has something to say to Jesus, and everyone knows to stay out of her way. She needs no help speaking her mind. Mary, on the other hand, is more tender. Her emotions are more easily discerned. People do not mind consoling gentle Mary; in fact, they feel compelled to protect and comfort her. But no one needs to protect Martha. Her strong will masks her brokenness. She dries her eyes, holds up her head, and goes out to meet Jesus.

"Lord, if you had been here, my brother would not have died" *(John 11:21).*

For the second time, she is accusing Jesus of not caring. After all, He did not do things her way or according to her plan. In response to her accusation, Jesus, graciously adjusts Martha—again. He redirects her focus, shifting her gaze from the death of her brother to the hope of the Messiah,

"I am the resurrection and the life; he who believes in Me shall live even if he dies, and everyone who lives and believes in Me shall never die. Do you believe this" *(John 11:25-26)?*

Martha relents—for a moment. Martha is so accustomed to being in charge; she cannot seem to realize Jesus does not need her advice or her help. After an emotional conversation with Mary, Jesus goes to the tomb of Lazarus. He orders the stone to be removed from the entrance. Martha butts in.

"Lord, by this time there will be a stench; for he has been dead four days" *(John 11:39).*

My mouth is agape when I read that verse. My imagination hears a little sarcasm or a passive-aggressive tone to her words. She is letting Jesus know if He had just done what she asked—days ago—they wouldn't be in this dilemma. *For heaven's sake, Jesus, you waited so long to get here, his body stinks!* Martha is still trying to have her say because she still believes she is right. She is still a little miffed at Jesus. She is telling Jesus what He should and shouldn't do. Martha has no idea what is about to happen.

While her remarks throughout John 11 may seem to highlight Martha's negative attributes, her responses to Jesus are simply the downside of her leadership traits. This woman has grit, tenacity, and confidence. Jesus has to refocus and redirect her strong will over and over, but when push comes to shove, when life is hard, when circumstances are overwhelming—Martha is the woman I want in my corner. So why does Martha struggle so often with her God-given personality? Perhaps the greater question is—why do we?

Why the Struggle?

Make no mistake. God created Martha to be a strong woman. He created Mary to be intuitive and sensitive. An elementary study of human psychology reveals we each have dominant God-given personality traits that motivate, direct, and affect everything about us. But why then do we struggle with the negative side of our divinely created personalities? Why does it seem the inherent weaknesses of our temperament take a front seat more often than we desire?

Scripture is clear. We are all related to Adam, and through that relationship, we inherit a sinful nature (Romans 5:18-19). We do not *become sinners* when we first commit an act of sin. *We are born sinners, therefore, we sin.* It is our nature. Our bent. Our leaning—no matter what our personality type (Ephesians 2:1-3). We are born into this world as children of Adam, and because of it, all have sinned (Romans 3:23). However, even after we come into the family of God by new

132

birth, we continue to struggle with sin. Our sin nature, our fleshly nature, is not eradicated when we become Christians. The Apostle Paul writes prolifically about his struggle with the sinful nature in Romans 7:14-25. The same struggle is real for every child of God. In fact, every New Testament letter written to the church addresses the problem of sin within the church. Yet Scripture repeatedly emphasizes we are not to live under the dominion or control of sin.

"Therefore do not let sin reign in your mortal body that you should obey its lusts, and do not go on presenting the members of your body to sin as instruments of unrighteousness; but present yourselves to God as those alive from the dead, and your members as instruments of righteousness to God. For sin shall not be master over you..." (Romans 6:12-14a).

As believers in Christ we are not obligated to live according to the desires of our sinful nature—no matter how strong, how ingrained, or how accepted by society those sinful desires may be. We have a choice and a responsibility to live differently. We have hope.

What is Our Hope?

No matter where we fall in the wide spectrum of personality types, our hope for living a life pleasing to God is the indwelling Holy Spirit of Christ.

Teaching on the subject of the Holy Spirit has extremes and, in some cases, abuses. We must not be trapped by any doctrine that ignores the purpose of the Holy Spirit or distorts the manifestation of the Holy Spirit. The indwelling Spirit of Christ is vital for every believer because He is the energy and power source for victorious Christian living.

Ephesians 1:13 reminds us we are sealed with the Holy Spirit at the moment of salvation. His presence within us is evidence of a permanent transaction. He does not come and go in our lives, leaving when we sin and returning when we repent. Certainly, He can be quenched or grieved, but He cannot be removed. The very nature of His presence within us is based on the completed work of Christ and God's faithfulness to us—not our performance or our faithfulness to Him. Additionally, the Holy Spirit does not indwell us in increments (Ephesians 1:3). We get all of Him the moment we are born into the family of God. It does, however, take a lifetime of learning to live in daily surrender to His control.

"Do not be drunk with wine, which leads to debauchery. Instead, be filled with the Spirit" (Ephesians 5:18 NIV).

We often conclude that being filled with the Holy Spirit is similar to an empty glass being filled with liquid. We are not empty, however, because the Spirit indwells us permanently. Therefore, Paul's contrasting analogy in Ephesians 5:18 is an admonition about control. The verb tense of the phrase *be filled* indicates a continuous action. The words *be filled* are also an imperative command with *you* as the unwritten, but understood, subject of the command. Living under the control of the Holy Spirit is not just for the super Christian; it's for you and me.

The contrast to strong drink is a picture of influence. Whatever we are under the influence of—controls us. Therefore, we are to live under the influence of the Holy Spirit. While He is always indwelling the believer, the believer chooses to surrender daily to His control. This choice is a day-by-day, moment-by-moment submission of our will to His. Remarkably, the Holy Spirit will give us the desire, as well as the ability, to surrender to Him (Philippians 2:13). The late Dr. Wayne Barber often said, "God will equip us to live as He has commanded us to live."

I am always hesitant to give lists or acronyms that

appear to be formulas for successful Christian living. I do, however, want spiritual principles to be easily understood and applicable. The daily filling of the Holy Spirit is a lifestyle we learn by practicing Biblical principles. The following list of words is not a recipe for success. It is an organized approach to help us remember truth as we seek a life controlled by the Holy Spirit.

Acknowledge. We must daily acknowledge our need for the Holy Spirit. We must recognize we cannot live the Christian life in abundance without Him and we are powerless to accomplish anything of lasting eternal value apart from Him. Like a deer panting for water, our soul—our innermost being—yearns for the influence and control of the Holy Spirit in every aspect and in every moment of life (Psalm 42:1).

Abandon. We abandon our sin. We allow the Lord to examine our lives with the spotlight of God's Word, asking His Spirit to convict and clean out anything that disrupts our relationship with God. We have already explored 1 John 1:9 several times. Memorize it and implement it daily—maybe even hourly.

Abdicate. We willingly give up control of our own lives. We surrender, submitting ourselves completely to the Lord. We abandon our will for His and we die to self." *I have been crucified with Christ; but it is no longer I who live, but Christ lives in me; and the life which I now live in the flesh I live by faith in the Son of God, who loved me and delivered Himself up for me"* (Galatians 2:20). That rotten old sin nature we are born with must die daily. The Holy Spirit enables us to die daily to self as we submit to Him.

Ask. We often overlook the obvious. We must ask for the filling of the Holy Spirit. We do not have to beg for it, plead for it, or bargain for it. It is ours for the asking—so ask.

Accept. Unfortunately, the filling of the Holy Spirit has been carelessly associated with all sorts of overt signs, odd behavior, and altered states of consciousness. Being controlled by God's Spirit is not dramatic behavior; instead, it is part of normal, healthy, everyday Christian living. It is the blessed routine of living in our privilege as children of God. We must not wait for supernatural feelings or signs to prove we are under the control of the Holy Spirit. We accept by faith that God will do what He has promised to do, and then we simply get up and live.

Make no mistake. There is indeed visible evidence of the Holy Spirit's work and control in the life of a believer. While some boldly espouse a filling of the Holy Spirit, the everyday rub of people and circumstances will quickly reveal its authenticity. Biblical evidence of the Holy Spirit cannot be contrived or counterfeited for long periods of time. It is easy to put on a spiritual show at church. It is hard to go to Walmart or drive in traffic or deal with difficult people and still behave like a child of God without daily surrender to the control of the Holy Spirit. In fact, it is impossible.

The greatest evidence of the Holy Spirit in the life of a believer is not signs and wonders. It is the fruit of the Spirit. *"But the fruit of the Spirit is love, joy, peace, patience, kindness, goodness, faithfulness, gentleness, self-control; against such things there is no law" (Galatians 5:22-23).*

Notice the word *fruit* is singular. Each word in the list is a qualifier of the fruit. We do not get to pick and choose from the qualifiers. I understand some people, some temperaments, seem to gravitate easily toward these characteristics. The problem is you and I cannot see the inner struggles or the heart of a person. Also, we often define these qualifiers by our own standard of measure instead of the Lord's. But keep in mind, while we cannot change our God-given temperament, we can, by the grace of God and the indwelling Holy Spirit, change our thinking, our behavior, and our outlook.

The Holy Spirit within us always points to Jesus. He never magnifies the flesh and certainly never calls attention to an individual—only to Christ (John 16:4). Anytime believers divert the focus away from Christ and onto themselves, the flesh has taken charge. For those of us who speak, teach, sing, or publically lead in any way, we must constantly be on guard. Without even realizing it, we can become the center of attention, enjoying the limelight, and quenching the Holy Spirit immediately. Actually, the struggle is real for every believer because the flesh is always selfish and self-serving. Our walk with Christ requires a constant listening for His gentle, but sometimes firm, readjustment of our hearts, minds, and behavior. Living under the control of the Holy Spirit is not a one-and-done, quiet-time event. It is a moment-by-moment surrender throughout each and every day.

Paul elaborates on the evidence of the Spirit-filled life in Ephesians 5:18-21. In fact, the final three chapters of Ephesians emphasize the effect our relationship with Christ has on others. The degree to which we surrender to the work of the Holy Spirit is the degree to which we will impact and bless people around us. A surrendered life is marked by thankfulness, joy, and submission. Don't run from the word submission. Even Jesus submitted to the Father. Submission does not minimize us or make us doormats. It does, however, allow us operate freely and joyfully wherever the Lord chooses to place us, honoring Him while blessing others.

"And do not be drunk with wine, for that is dissipation, but be filled with the Spirit, speaking to one another in psalms and hymns and spiritual songs, singing and making melody with your hearts to the Lord; always giving thanks for all things in the name of our Lord Jesus Christ, to God, even the Father; and be subject to one another in the fear [reverence] of Christ" (Ephesians 5:18-21).

So what happened to Martha?

The third and final time we meet Mary and Martha,

Scripture says only four words about Martha. But, oh, those four words speak volumes.

...and Martha was serving... (John 12:2).

There are no strong words from Martha, and no adjustment from Jesus. Something has changed...in Martha.

The resurrection of Lazarus in John 11 is a turning point in Jesus' ministry as well as in Martha's life. The power over life and death has drawn a line in the sand for everyone—for religious leaders, disciples, and believers like Martha. Jesus has unequivocally proven He is God, and there can be no waffling about who is in control. Martha finally understands that her words, her plans, and her desires must forever be surrendered to His. When we find Martha serving in John 12:2, Jesus has not changed her personality or her giftedness; neither has He dismissed her skills and abilities. Instead, Martha has learned to surrender, and with both awe and contentment—she serves.

Mary's actions are more notable than Martha's in John 12. Mary causes quite a stir with her beautiful, tender, emotional outpouring of love. She anoints the feet of Jesus and then wipes His feet with her hair. It is such a Mary moment. But notice what is *not* happening. Martha is not complaining about Mary's absence in the kitchen. Martha is content taking up the slack in the kitchen and seeing to the guests, but *she is also content to let Mary be Mary*. Don't get me wrong. I'm fairly sure Martha has organized the other women, decided on the menu, and delegated jobs at this pre-Passover gathering. Her personality and abilities have not changed. They have been surrendered. In doing so, not only is Martha serving in freedom, but Mary is able to serve in freedom as well. Both Martha and Mary are anchored. They are living in the hope—Jesus can use every personality for His purpose and His glory.

I read an internet quote by author and speaker Patsy Clairmont. She hits the nail on the head.

I'm drawn to calm people. Not vacant, like the light is on, but nobody's home. Not arrogant as if they are holding tight to the reins of control. I'm drawn instead to those who exude settledness and centeredness. Their insides aren't churning, their tongues are not wagging. They aren't fretting, stewing, and clamoring. They are functioning in their gifts and they are not threatened by yours. They are anchored in Christ and the sea within them is still. I find that kind of steadiness compelling.

I have a dear friend who is a Martha. I met her at church when she attended one of my Bible studies. We became friends almost immediately. Looking back, I am confident she is an example of God's anticipatory love for me. He knew I would need a Martha—through cancer, through book writing, through teaching, through struggles. My friend, Trina, can accomplish more in one day than I can in a week. She is a doer and a motivator. At times, she goes with me when I teach in other churches. While there, she carries books and supplies, often reminding me of people's names. She handles details I easily forget or do not see. She makes it possible for me to concentrate on teaching, sometimes getting the accolades, while she humbly serves. Make no mistake; Trina is vastly gifted, a purposeful leader, and infinitely invested in countless people. At this particular time, however, I am thankful for her investment in me. Sometimes, I am a Mary, but I cannot be a Mary without a Martha somewhere in my life. In this season, Trina is my Martha.

Dear reader, there is no perfect personality type. Neither Martha nor Mary is better than the other. We are all divinely created yet filled with flaws because sin has marred us. Yet there is hope for each of us, and as always our hope is

Jesus Christ. The indwelling of His Holy Spirit transforms our God-given temperaments into instruments of righteousness, usable for His divine purpose. Our responsibility is to yield to His control—to surrender. It is our hope and also our choice. Whether you are a Mary or a Martha, choose to live in your hope.

Discussion Questions

1. Would you describe yourself as more of a Mary or a Martha? What are the advantages and disadvantages? No matter if we relate more to Mary or to Martha, why do we often struggle with the negative side of our personalities?

2. Discuss this statement, "We cannot change our personality, but we can change our behavior." For the believer in Christ, why is this true?

3. How can a Christian live daily under the control of the Holy Spirit? Review and discuss the five "A's" in this chapter (Acknowledge, Abandon, Abdicate, Ask, Accept).

4. What evidence will there be in our lives if we are under the control of the Holy Spirit? (Read Galatians 5:22-23, Ephesians 5:18-21)

5. In Christ, how can people with opposite personality types complement one another and help one another? Can you give an example from your own life?

WOMEN OF HOPE

7

THE SAMARITAN WOMAN
Hope for the Shamed

Jesus said, *"I came that they might have life, and might have it abundantly"* (John 10:10b). Certainly, we all want to experience abundant life, but unfortunately for many, a seemingly impenetrable barrier stands in the way. Shame.

Shame chains us to the past. It blinds us to the future. It tries to extinguish hope and steal our joy and peace. Shame, no matter how it wormed itself into our lives, can be a powerful weapon in the arsenal of the enemy, attempting to defeat us. Yet Jesus didn't come to gloss over our shame. He came to shatter it.

The gospel of John presents a woman who is well acquainted with shame. She is caught in a lifestyle perhaps driven by shame and certainly resulting in it. She does not foresee the mundane chore of drawing water from a well translating into vibrant, new life. But Jesus does. He waits for her, and every other woman caught in the grip of shame, offering abundant life and abundant hope.

Divine Appointment

It was a traveler's nightmare. I was taking five other women from Illinois to Nicaragua to lead a retreat for English-speaking workers. Our flight out of St. Louis was delayed. Then cancelled. We were re-routed to Miami through Chicago on a much later flight. On the unexpected flight from Chicago to Miami, my seat assignment was separated from the other ladies in my group. Instead of sitting with my friends, I was seated next to a lovely young woman. My spirit had a catch.

The lovely woman seated to my left was an international finance expert. She and her husband lived on the West Coast. We covered the pleasantries of conversation in the first ten minutes of the flight, and then she asked about the group I had boarded with. I explained who we were and what we were doing in Nicaragua. Immediately, the conversation took a turn.

I learned she had been in New York City in the North Tower of the World Trade Center on September 11, 2001, when an airplane crashed into the building. I learned of her escape and of the loss of her co-workers. Her eyes glazed as she spoke. She and her husband had moved cross-country in an effort to leave behind the memories, start a new life, and search for peace. I asked, "Have you found it?" She replied, "No."

For the remainder of the flight, we talked of brokenness and hope, searching and Christ. Our plane landed and she gave me her business card. A few weeks later, I wrote her a letter and included a copy of the book *Purpose Driven Life*. Although I never heard back from my fellow passenger, I will forever believe the unplanned travel debacles were all part of God's plan—arranged for one wounded woman searching for peace and desperately in need of hope.

Jesus has a divine appointment with another wounded woman, an unnamed Samaritan woman He encounters at a well. We find her story in John 4.

The account is the longest recorded conversation Jesus has with any person in the New Testament, and that He has this conversation with a Samaritan woman is intriguing. Countless sermons covering a myriad of topics have been preached about Jesus' encounter with this woman, but my heart wants to know who she is. What pain is driving her to draw water in the noonday heat? As a woman, what does Scripture want me to see in her brokenness? For the unnamed Samaritan woman and for every other person searching for peace...

Hope is waiting.

Jesus and His disciples leave Judea to head north into Galilea. The conundrum of Samaria lies in between (John 4:3-4). The Jews hated the Samaritans and would normally take an alternate route to avoid the region altogether. The hatred had festered for centuries, and in Jesus' day a common Jewish prayer was for *no Samaritan to be in the resurrection*. In other words, *may all Samaritans go to hell*. Pretty strong hatred. But why?

After King Solomon's reign, the nation of Israel was divided (1 Kings 12:1-24). Unhappy with King Rehoboam's high taxes and forced labor, the ten northern tribes of Israel rebelled and pulled away to form a new nation of Israel. Jeroboam became their king making Samaria the new capital city. From this point forward in Old Testament history, the ten northern tribes are called Israel and the two southern tribes are called Judah.

Jeroboam strengthened the identity of the northern

tribes by instituting a false system of worship. He didn't want them returning to Jerusalem to worship God for fear they would return to King Rehoboam as well (1 Kings 12:25-33). Jeroboam deceptively intertwined Judaism and idolatry. He fashioned golden calves to worship and placed them at opposite ends of the new kingdom for easy access. Furthermore, he instituted a false priesthood and pagan festivals. The northern tribes relished it all. God eventually judged them for their disobedience.

Judgement came through the Assyrians (2 Kings 17:5-7). God allowed this fierce world power not only to capture the northern kingdom of Israel but also to deconstruct it.

Assyria maintained an iron grip on the nations it conquered by importing and exporting captured people. They would mix up the nations—moving people from one captured region into a completely different captured region. This mixing of people groups prevented nationalistic bonds from forming, thus destroying anything that might bind people together or inspire uprisings. Eventually, these relocated people groups would intermarry and have families, creating entirely new races and new cultures.

The Samaritans were a byproduct of Assyria's methods. By Jewish standards, Samaritans were half-breeds: once rebellious Jews who were judged by God, conquered by Assyria, intermarried with pagans, and ultimately viewed as the dogs of society—forever cursed and vehemently hated.

Yet the Bible says *Jesus **had** to pass through Samaria* (John 4:4).

Certainly, there was another route that would take Jesus and His disciples around the despised region, but Jesus was compelled to go through Samaria. He *had* to go. He knew He had a divine appointment with a Samaritan woman at a well. The well is Jacob's well, a place rich in Jewish history. More importantly, the well has the finest, most refreshing water in the entire region. The time is noon. By the Jewish clock the sixth hour is the middle of the day. It is hot and not a normal time for drawing water. The only person at the well is Jesus. Other than withdrawing to pray, it is one of the few times in Scripture He is alone. The disciples have gone to buy food while the Lord simply sits down and waits –for her. He knows she is coming, but she has no idea joy is just ahead. For this obscure woman, life is about to change because Hope is waiting at the well.

Do you see the divine fingerprint of God in this encounter? Do you see the plans of Jesus sovereignly orchestrated for one precious woman? Dear one, Jesus has a divine appointment with you as well. He will meet you in the mundane busyness of life. He will push through and push aside all the distractions and noise to wait for your arrival. Like the Samaritan woman, joy is just ahead. Will you sit with Him and be refreshed? Will you tune your heart to hear His hope?

Divine Deliverance

Jesus knows the woman has a great need. Of course, she thinks her need is fresh water, but Jesus knows her greatest need is forgiveness and deliverance from shame. He begins the conversation with what seems like a simple request for a drink of water from Jacob's well. The request, however, is anything but simple.

The Samaritan woman is shocked by Jesus' request for a drink. She is a woman and Jewish men do not carry on casual conversations with women. Furthermore, she is Samaritan woman. A Jewish man would typically avoid her as if she were a mongrel dog, and certainly no Jew would ever receive a drink from her. But Jesus has no cup to drink from. He has no bucket to draw water with. He is completely dependent on her utensils if he wants a taste of cool refreshing water.

And there it is. The first layer of shame is revealed. Using *her* cup or *her* jar of water will render Jesus ceremonially unclean by Jewish religious standards. Simply

147

because she was born into this apostate people group, she feels the weight of generational sin—not her personal sin at this juncture, but the sin of her people. She recalls the hatred and the condemnation that has been passed down through the centuries and has somehow been laid squarely on her shoulders—just because. It is not her fault. It is not her personal shame. It is shame that has been placed upon her from outside circumstances. This woman understands that to a Jew not only her cup and her water jar are unclean but also *she* is unclean and condemned. Shame seeps out.

Jesus' request carries no condemnation, but the woman cannot fathom His compassion, and her reply bites. *"How is it that you, being a Jew, ask me for a drink since I am a Samaritan woman?"* There is defensiveness and even resentment in her response. The shame of her heritage causes her to put up her guard. The hurt masquerades as pride. Jesus sees it all and begins a conversation that draws her in.

He talks with her of common things like water. He does not verbally berate her with laws and rules and theology. He converses in an uncontrived manner. He speaks about the regular things of life. His calm kindness engages her. She listens to the fascinating prospect of living water and the possibility of never thirsting again. Her heart aches for it as she leans in to listen (John 4:10).

Jesus digs deeper. While water is certainly refreshing, it also cleanses, and Jesus knows this Samaritan woman needs cleansing. Her personal sin must be confronted and her personal shame must be removed. After all, she has come to a well at noon, avoiding an encounter even with other Samaritans. What on earth could she have done to desire such isolation?

"Go call your husband and come here" (John 4:16).

148

Jesus' second request causes her to stiffen. He hits a nerve. No accusation. No threat. No pointed finger. Just a direct request that goes straight to her heart. Her reply is equally straightforward.

"*I have no husband*" (John 4:17).

My sanctified imagination wonders how many years of heartache are wrapped in those four words. How much sorrow is buried in her reply? This is an unusual man, engaging in unusual conversation, and now making an unusual request. His words cut her like a knife. Shame no longer seeps. It gushes.

Jesus has no intention of brushing aside her shame. In fact, he wants to unearth it. In the process, He does not condemn her but instead commends her for her honest summation of the facts. "*You have well said, 'I have no husband'; for you have had five husbands; and the one whom you now have is not your husband; this you have said truly*" (John 4:17b-18).

Five husbands. The implication is not five marriages because she was widowed; rather it is five marriages that ended in divorce. For the Jews, two divorces were acceptable and for the Samaritans three divorces were acceptable. But five? Nobody, not even Samaritans, would turn a blind eye to five.

What possible reason could there be for such disastrous marriages? Was she a serial adulteress? Was she careless or perhaps unlucky in love? Was she caught in the cycle of abuse? Was she a needy, empty woman seeking to find fulfillment in men—and never found it? Undeterred, Jesus, like a skilled surgeon cutting out a cancer, exposes her sin and consequently exposes her shame. Whatever the reasons or the circumstances for her lifestyle, shame is the byproduct. After all, she is at a well. At noon. Hiding.

What is shame and where does it come from?

The Hebrew word for *shame* is *bosh.* In its root form, it means *"to become pale* or *to blush."* Dr. Spiros Zodiates writes, *"When failure or sin occurs, there is a disconcerted feeling, a flushing of the face, humiliation and shattered human emotion"* (The Key Word Study Bible*).* The creation account in Genesis takes us back to the very beginning when shame entered the world.

The Bible says God created Adam and Eve and in the purity of undefiled creation, they were naked and unashamed (Genesis 2:25). Unfortunately, marital bliss was short lived. Genesis 3 records the fateful conversation between Eve and the serpent and the subsequent disobedience of both Adam and Eve.

The serpent, Satan the deceiver, engages Eve in a conversation and Eve responds. He casts doubt on the goodness of God when he asks, *"Indeed, has God said, 'You shall not eat from any tree of the garden'?"* Stop right there. Satan knew good and well what God had said. He is not trying to clarify information. He is trying to confuse and deceive.

Deception can be defined as *"causing someone to believe a lie."* It is Satan's mode of operation. He does not always speak obvious lies. Sometime he whispers doubt, manipulating truth with confusion. Eve thinks she is up for the task of setting the serpent straight. So instead of walking away from the conversation she has already begun, she replies, giving the answer her husband has relayed to her based on God's instruction *(Genesis 2:16-17).*

In conversing with the serpent, however, Eve misspeaks. She relates the truth that they are not to eat from the tree in the middle of the garden, BUT she adds they are not to touch it as well. Certainly, touching it might lead to wanting it, but God never said anything about touching it. She added something God never said. Not only does she add to God's

150

Word, but she softens it, telling the serpent that disobedience *might* lead to death (Genesis 3:3). God was clear in Genesis 2:17. Disobedience will **surely** lead to death but Eve takes it down a notch. After all, *"you shall surely die"* sounds a little harsh to her.

Satan pounces. *"You surely shall not die!"* Initially he casts doubt on the goodness of God causing confusion in Eve's mind. Now he blatantly calls God a liar. The serpent accuses God of holding out on Adam and Eve, of depriving them of something better, of being less than a good and loving Father. Satan spits out the lie, *"For God knows that in the day you eat from it your eyes will be opened, and **you will be like God**, knowing good from evil"* (Genesis 3:5).

Oh, dear one, quickly examine that lie, *"...you will be like God...."* Those are the very words that began a great war in Heaven (Revelation 12:9). They are the words that expelled Lucifer from God's presence for eternity (Isaiah 14:14). They are the heartbeat of pride, the great sin of Satan, the destructive illusion that our ways, our thoughts, and our desires are higher, better, and more noble than God's. God always responds aggressively toward pride (James 4:6). It is the root of all sin, and in Genesis 3, Satan is perpetuating his sin onto mankind. *And Eve believed the lie.*

Eve took the fruit, ate it, and then gave it to her husband to eat. Immediately, their eyes were open. They saw their nakedness and they were ashamed (Genesis 3:7). Shame was the unforeseen consequence of sin. It still is. Along with unbelief and fear (Genesis 3:8-10), shame was forever established in the arsenal of Satan.

Dr. David Powilson, CEO of Christian Counseling and Educational Foundation, gives an apt description of shame. "Guilt is the awareness of failure to a standard. Shame is the sense of failure in the eyes of someone." Shame is relational. It is not simply missing the mark, but it is failing in someone else's estimation. Interestingly, shame can indeed come from our own sin, but it can also be placed on us from an outside source. John Piper calls this kind of shame "misplaced shame." A family secret, someone else's sin, someone else's opinion, or what someone else has done to us can produce misplaced shame.

Make no mistake, shame is a weapon of our enemy. Scripture calls him a murderer and the father of lies (John 8:44). He is the tempter (Matthew 4:3), the evil one (Matthew 13:19), and the accuser of the brethren (Revelation 12:10). His name is Satan, which means adversary. He is called the devil, meaning slanderer. Ephesians 2:1-3 and Ephesians 6:1-10 tells us he is a formidable enemy who will unpack his arsenal of unbelief, fear, and shame in any way, shape, or form that keeps us from God. When shame is the weapon of choice, the enemy does not care about the origin of our shame. He does not care if it is shame from our personal sin or if it is misplaced shame. He simply wants to keep us in it.

`Why is shame such an effective weapon? What does it do to us?

Shame will make us feel defeated. It will cause us to run from God. It will keep us from His Word and pull us away from other Christians. Shame will hinder the work of the Holy Spirit in our lives. It will render our ministry unfruitful and unfulfilling. Shame will attempt to steal our peace and our joy. Shame can even drive us back to the very sin that caused the shame, somehow seeking momentary relief from the shame.

Shame can push us to opposite ends of the behavioral spectrum. It can cause us to be self-deprecating and produce in us a sense of worthlessness. It can rob us of daily productivity, and it can manifest itself in depression and despondency. On the other hand, shame can create brashness and a bravado that seeks to cover up the shame. Busyness can become a distraction from the shame. Even perfectionism can be an attempt to rise above it.

Shame works because it keeps us from living in victory, and Satan will use it to beat us to a pulp. But it is NEVER, NEVER, NEVER God's plan or God's intention for us to live in shame.

This is a difficult chapter to write. I have seen the devastation shame produces in the lives of others. I have listened to repugnant stories of abuse from innocent victims and realized shame is the bully stick keeping the innocent from freedom. I know women who stay in harmful relationships because shame has convinced them it is all their fault and hope is not an option. The shame of addictions, habits, and secret sin has shackled Christians and non-Christians to a life of bottomless guilt.

There was a time in my own life when I stood to speak or teach in front of an unfamiliar crowd, and shame whispered in my ear. I would hear the daunting accusation that someone out there knew something about my imperfect past. For years, the accessible world of social media terrified me. What if someone hears me teaching and that person could rightly speak a word of condemnation about me? What if ....? Today, in these later years of life, people sometimes comment about my openness when I teach. While I spare the disparaging details, I am convinced that exposing darkness to the light of Christ crushes any weapon Satan might form against me (Isaiah 54:17).

Oh, precious reader, shame will attempt to silence us. It wants to keep our sin and our sorrows in the shadows. It will make every effort to suffocate freedom. It will diminish our view of a blessed future because it only showcases the failures of our past. The greatest desire of shame is to extinguish hope, but hope cannot be defeated or extinguished. Hope will not be silenced. Hope holds the key to every shame-filled chain. Listen to the song of hope resounding throughout Scripture!

Our hope is in Christ Jesus.

Ephesians 2:1-3 is perhaps the best description of our spiritual condition before we meet Christ. It speaks of our enemy, our fallen world, and our own personal sinful nature. *"But God."* Verse four starts with the sweetest words in all of Scripture. It denotes a change of direction, a contrast to the grim truth of the preceding verses. God steps into the most hopeless of situations and provides hope. That hope is Jesus Christ.

When we read Ephesians 2:4-5, we will not see condemnation or shame. The overwhelming message is grace, mercy, and love offered to us through Jesus. Let your heart soak in the beauty and the hope of the gospel.

*"**But God,** being rich in mercy, because of His great love with which He loved us, even when we were dead in our transgressions, made us alive together with Christ. By grace you have been saved."*

The truth and illustration presented in Colossians 2:13-15 further confirms our hope in Christ. Paul is clear: we are without hope when we are without Christ. In fact the list of decrees against us is endless. He uses the illustration of a debtor in verse 14 of Colossians 2.

In the Roman world, when a person accrued debt he could not pay, his creditors made a humiliating list of the debts. Often the debtor was thrown into prison until the debt could be paid or the creditors satisfied. The debtor's entire family bore the burden of repaying impossible debt. The shame of the debtor's plight was exacerbated by nailing the list of debts to the doorpost of his home for everyone to see. Few debtors ever recovered from the weight or the stigma of such debt.

Paul likens our spiritual condition before knowing Christ to that of the ancient debtor. The debt of sin is impossible to pay. The guilt and shame is too burdensome to relieve. *"But God"* steps into our hopelessness of debt and provides the payment through Jesus. Calvary is the doorpost to which our sin is nailed. Jesus not only paid the debt with His life, He also bore the shame of it with His death. His payment settles our sin debt for eternity.

The writer of Hebrews tells us Christ *"endured the cross, despising the shame"* (Hebrews 12:2). He did not dismiss the shame or ignore the shame or downplay the shame. He endured every part of the cross for our benefit—even the shame of it. Furthermore, His resurrection is the victorious triumph over anyone or anything who would attempt to shackle us with the shame of debt again (Colossians 2:15).

Exuberantly, Paul writes, *"There is therefore now no condemnation for those who are in Christ Jesus"* (Romans 8:1). Condemnation means *no hope*. Because of the death and resurrection of Christ, we do not live as hopeless people, condemned, with no way out. Dear one, the opposite is true. We have hope. We have Christ.

Romans 8 ends with a climactic trilogy of questions. Paraphrased, Romans 8:33-39 reads like this:

Who can bring a charge against God's people? Only God and He won't!

Who can condemn us? Only Christ and He will not!

Who can separate us from the love of God through Christ? No one and nothing. NOT EVEN SHAME!

For those of us who have experienced shame, hope permeates Scripture. But as with every gift of grace given to us through Christ, we must receive it. We must trust God, believing the spiritual blessings belong to us in Christ. We must unwrap and use every gift. When the enemy seeks to assault us with unbelief, fear, and shame, we must, in the power of the Holy Spirit, STAND FIRM.

Ephesians 6:10-20 are powerful verses about living in freedom. Three times in these verses, Paul writes, "*Stand Firm.*" It means "*to hold your position at a critical time of battle.*" What is our position? What battle?

Our position is one of right standing with God. It is all God has said we are in Christ Jesus. The first three chapters of Ephesians relate the blessings and the benefits of knowing Christ.

Sought by God (Ephesians 1:4-6).

Saved by grace through faith (Ephesians 1:6-7, 2:4-5, 2:8-9).

Sealed with the Holy Spirit (Ephesians 1:13-14).

Seated at the table of God as a member of God's family (Ephesians 2:6 and 19).

Strengthened in the inner man by the Holy Spirit (Ephesians 3:16-19).

Our battle is a spiritual battle, initiated by our enemy Satan. He will attempt to use his age-old arsenal of unbelief, fear, and shame, but his tactical plan of attack will be based on your particular weaknesses and bents (Ephesians 6:11). Scripture says when the enemy attacks, STAND FIRM. Do not believe the lie of the enemy. Do not succumb to fear. Do not let shame have a foothold. You are a child of the Most High. Stand in the truth. Live in the truth. Speak the truth. This is how we hold our position in the heat of spiritual warfare. *Stand firm* is not an option. It is a command. **However, spiritual victory is not typically a dramatic encounter with the demonic. Instead, it is a day-by-day choice to live in obedience to Christ.**

Do you see it? Will you let the truth soak into your heart and mind? We are not obligated to live in shame! It is not ours to carry. Christ took our sin as well as our shame (no matter how we got it), depositing them into hell for eternity. Live daily in that truth. There is freedom in it!

The following email came from a fellow cancer survivor who heard me teach on the subject of shame. It is one of the most powerful emails I have ever received.

I have carried a cloak of shame for so many years about so many things, that until the lesson the other night, I thought I would be buried in it. Recently, I have felt it slip off from time to time, but I never let go of it. That cloak was woven of things I did, things I did not do, and things others have done to me. The shame I have carried was truly suffocating me and killing me as sure as any cancer. It turned me into someone I was not. When you said the word [shame], tears came to my eyes.

I have come to understand that I am forgiven. I cannot tell you the joy that has brought me. That I could be forgiven. God could love and forgive ME. That concept left me long ago if I ever understood it in the first place. I have hope. God's grace is for me too.

Last week, after hearing about Jesus and the woman at the well, again, I was overcome with joy. I can throw off this damn cloak of shame that I have carried for so long. I can trust God's promises for ME. I cannot tell you what that means to me. I am sobbing as I write this.

Divine Results

So what happened to the woman at the well?

Jesus has exposed her sin and her shame without condemnation or ridicule. She is disconcerted if not shaken by His knowledge of her life. She even calls Him a prophet (John 4:19). But instead of allowing the Lord to free her and certainly before He dredges up any other unpleasantry about her life— she sidesteps. She does what many of us do when we want to sound spiritual, but are unwilling to examine our own lives. She changes the subject and talks about religion. And Jesus lets her talk.

Many sermons have been preached about worship using John 4:20-25 as the text. There is a great amount of doctrine packed into this portion of their conversation. Yet somehow I imagine Jesus calmly smiling, letting her talk, while also answering her rather accusatory question about worship. Jesus knows this is a divine appointment. He knows no matter what she chooses to talk about, the conversation will eventually come back around to her life, her need, her sin, and her shame. It only takes four verses before she realizes this religious conversation is going nowhere. She doesn't even understand what Jesus is talking about.

Religion never satisfies the hunger of the heart. In fact, it only adds to it. Yet the topic of religion, church, or denominationalism is a much more palatable conversation than one about Jesus. When I travel and sit next to someone who is willing to converse, I rarely tell them what I do for a living. Most people would rather chew their arm off than talk to a Bible teacher. But if they discover what I do and they are still willing to converse, religion is the safest subject.

The Samaritan woman, however, wearies quickly of religious conversation and with a heavy sigh, defers to the coming Messiah to make all things known (John 4:25). To the modern-day reader, there is nothing spectacular about her heavy- hearted statement, but to Jesus it is the divine turning point in the conversation.

Samaritans did not believe in a Jewish Messiah. They did not teach or believe the entire Old Testament. They only had the Pentateuch, the first five books of the Old Testament. They did not embrace the writings of the prophets or the wisdom literature of Solomon or the songs of David. They were not familiar with the prophecies of the coming Messiah. They did not sing the prophetic psalms. They had no hope of a Deliverer. Yet here is a Samaritan woman into whom God Himself has planted a divine yearning for the Messiah. It is that divine yearning which has led her to this well, on this day, and to this unusual man. And into that yearning, Jesus speaks.

"I who speak to you am He"(John 4:26).

All of eternity stands still. In the holy hush between verses 26 and 27, God's Spirit is working. He is pulling together the pieces of the day. The weary task of drawing water at noon, hiding from her own countrymen. The unusual man asking for a drink. The prospect of living water. The probing request about her husband. The perplexing conversation about worship. And now, the stunning words that Jesus has never uttered to anyone and will never utter again until he stands trial, *"I am He."*

In the silent pause when Heaven itself is poised for celebration, understanding dawns. Her eyes fill with tears. Her chin quivers. Messiah *has* come and He is standing right in front of her, pouring out compassion. To Him, she is not a dirty Samaritan. Neither is she a hopeless sinner. The shame placed on her from the outside and the shame generated from within dissipate. The cloak of shame drops. She is forgiven. She is free.

Will you sit still for a moment and feel her freedom? Wrap your heart and mind around the lightness of soul grace and hope bring to her. Do you need the same release? Do you long to drink the blessing of forgiveness and taste for yourself its freedom from the weight of shame? Do you need to embrace the wonderful truth that misplaced shame is not yours to carry and no suffocating condemnation can deter the grace of Christ? Her freedom can be your freedom because Christ offers it to us all.

For Jesus and the Samaritan woman, that beautiful silent moment of realization is broken by those twelve clattering disciples returning from town with food (John 4:27). The disciples are amazed and probably disgusted to see Jesus conversing with her, but they say nothing to Jesus, the woman says nothing to them, and Jesus offers no explanation. Perhaps a knowing smile of mercy and thankfulness passes between the woman and Jesus. She backs away, eyes locked on the Lord. And then she runs.

The Bible is very specific about the direction of her running (John 4:28). She leaves the well and returns to her city to tell the good news of hope and forgiveness and freedom. But she does not go to her mother or her sisters or her girlfriends. *She goes to the men.* The men who know her well. The men who have probably told sordid stories or made off-color jokes about her. The men who have mocked her desperation. The men who know the names of her five husbands and the dismal circumstances surrounding each divorce.

Bursting with good news of the Messiah, she goes to these men. She does not convey the conversation about living water or the temple in Jerusalem or the proper place to worship. She blurts out the startling account, *"He told me all the things that I have done"* (John 4:29, 39). She is not hiding anymore. She is not bearing the shame anymore. In fact, she declares with freedom, *"Come and see."* And they came. For some of us, this chapter is a crossroad, a place to listen to

160

the probing questions of the Holy Spirit. Is this moment your divine appointment? Is today the day you will see compassion in the eyes of Jesus and the voice of condemnation will be silenced forever? Are you aching for the refreshing, cleansing, living water of Christ? Forgiveness is available for your personal sin and the shame it has fostered. But precious reader, freedom is also available from the misplaced shame you seem conscripted to carry. Christ is the victor over shame—no matter its source or the depths of its consequences.

In concluding the account of the woman at the well, Scripture says Jesus stayed in Samaria two days longer. A great spiritual awakening swept the region, and many Samaritans believed in Christ. John 4:39 says it began with one woman released from shame.

Do you see the results of forgiveness and freedom? Not only is one life changed but also many others. The same is true for our lives and our stories of freedom. The results are limitless. Our homes, our cities, and even our churches need to hear the good news of freedom and see the lives changed by Christ. Certainly, we are not compelled to share the details of our sin or our shame. However, a willingness to present ourselves as a testimony of redemption and grace offers hope to others.

I had casually met Helen several times and every time we ran into each other, I liked her! She is in ministry as well, and we seemed to have a lot in common. So, we finally set a time to have coffee and get better acquainted. I was looking forward to a refreshing, fun hour of ministry talk and light conversation. God had a different plan.

Thirty minutes into our delightful conversation, Helen asked how she could pray for me. I floundered and said something rather superficial, not wanting to wade too deeply into a new friendship. Helen, however, dove in.

"You know I have horrific sexual abuse in my past?"

She asked the question so matter-of-fact. No self-pity. No anger. And no, I did not know anything about her or her past—so she continued.

My new friend had experienced years of childhood sexual abuse at the hands of a family member. In her words, "I was abused every day of my life for ten long years." My jaw dropped and silent shock was her cue to tell the rest of her story.

When the abuse ended, Helen dealt with the ongoing trauma of it through harmful life choices. She was a Christian and attending church, even meeting her future husband through her church youth ministry. The shame of her past, however, had permeated and poisoned her mind. Not even her forthcoming marriage to a promising minister could undo the shame.

The jarring story of abuse and the calm, clear-eyed woman sitting before me were difficult to reconcile—but for Christ. Helen's healing has included extensive therapy and spiritual mentoring. There has been nothing instantaneous or easy about her road to freedom. Certainly, she carries scars, but the overwhelming truth I heard that afternoon was her realization the initial shame did not belong to her. It had been placed on her by someone else's sin. Additionally, her subsequent sinful choices were forgiven, and the shame of those choices abolished forever. In the beauty of freedom, she has been able to forgive her abuser. Although she has no contact with him, her release from shame is final and permanent. Why? Because Jesus came to give abundant life and that abundant life includes freedom from shame.

Not long ago, Helen shared her story at a large gathering of women. Afterwards, several women came to her in tears, telling similar stories and needing similar healing. Helen was able to point each of them to Christ, using her own life as validation. She was also able to offer resources and contacts to assist those women in their journey toward healing. To me, my

162

friend Helen is the embodiment of *"ashes to beauty"* (Isaiah 61:3).

Oh, I do not want to oversimplify the ravages of sin and the depths of shame some are carrying. But the truth of the gospel is so very simple: Christ has come to set us free. Freedom is the heart beat of the Gospel. *"Come and see"* is the beckoning call to anyone hiding beneath a cloak of shame. See what the Lord has done in countless lives. Taste the goodness of forgiveness and grace. Experience the healing only Christ can give. This is our hope in Christ. He longs to set us free.... even from shame.

Discussion Questions
Read John 4:3-41

1. Jesus had a divine appointment with a Samaritan wom-
    an who had a very messy life. Has there ever been a
    time when the Lord met you in the messiness of life?

2. Read Genesis 3:1-8. When and how did shame first en-
    ter the world? Why is it so effective even today?

3. Shame can come from our own sin or it can be placed
    on us from an outside source. Jesus deals with both
    sources. How does this give us hope and comfort?

4. Why do you think it is easier to talk with someone
    about religion than it is to talk about Jesus?

5. Read Romans 8:33-39. Thinking about your own life,
    how do these verses speak to you?

8

MARY MAGDALENE
Hope for Every Season

It was the 70s and *Jesus Christ Superstar* was a huge
Broadway success. One of the most popular songs from the
musical was written from Mary Magdalene's point of view.
The song spilled over to the pop music charts and even made
Billboard magazine's top 40. In fact, two versions of the song
were in the top forty at the same time--a rare occurrence,
confirming the popularity of the ballad. My high school
girls' chorus sang an arrangement of "*I Don't Know How to
Love Him.*" I loved that song! Unfortunately, the lyrics only
perpetuated the myths and falsehoods which have surrounded
Mary Magdalene for centuries.

So who is Mary Magdalene, according to Scripture?
What is the real story about her relationship with Christ? And
what can she teach us about hope?

Hope for the Past

Mary is a common name in Scripture. To distinguish this Mary from many others, she is called Mary Magdalene. Magdalene, however, is not her last name; rather it is a reference to her hometown, Magdala, a small fishing village in Galilee. Biblical writers attach the town to her first name, and originally it may have read Mary of Magdala or Mary the Magdalene.

Twice in Scripture, we are told Mary had seven demons cast from her by Christ. Both mentions are single verses with no details (Luke 8:2, Mark 16:9). It is all we know of her past. Therefore, to understand her state before she met Jesus, it would be reasonable to look at general characteristics of other demon-possessed people presented in Scripture. It is also important to understand what demon possession is and what it is not.

Revelation 12:7-9 tells of a great war in Heaven. Lucifer, a created angel of God, rebelled against God, and because of pride tried to usurp God's throne. God expelled Lucifer from Heaven. In the process of being defeated, the angels who sided with Lucifer were cast out as well. Those cast-down angels became demons. Lucifer became known as Satan, meaning *adversary*. This army of evil is real. It still exists. Like Satan, however, they are a defeated enemy, and one day both Satan and his demons will be cast into hell permanently.

Demon possession is presented in Scripture as a reality. It was not an ancient way of explaining physical or mental illness. Scripture distinguishes between illness and demon possession (Matthew 4:24). Certainly demon possession could manifest itself in physical and mental ailments (Matthew 12:22, Matthew 9:32-33, Luke 13:10-13), but in Scripture not all ailments are attributed to demon possession. Likewise, not all demon possession led to physical or mental ailments.

Moreover, Scripture is clear. Believers in Christ cannot be possessed by demons. The believer has the indwelling of the Holy Spirit. The Spirt of Christ and a demon cannot share the same space. A believer might be oppressed or harassed by demonic activity, but never possessed. Those who are indeed possessed by demons are unbelievers who do not know Christ.

In Scripture, a demon-possessed person does not seek out Christ. Either Jesus comes to them or someone else brings the possessed person to Jesus. Every demon recognizes Jesus' authority, and they obey without question. Mercifully, Jesus never condemns the possessed person or chastises them for their condition. He simply sets them free.

A Biblical examination of demon possession gives us a clearer image of the victim's plight. Perhaps the most dramatic account is that of the demoniac living among the tombs in Gerasene (Luke 8:26-39). The gospel of Mark records this account as well but refers to two men living in the tombs. The two accounts do not conflict. Luke simply focuses on one of the men.

The man in Gerasene had supernatural strength. He was often bound with chains and shackles, but somehow he was able to break free. Mark's account adds the man cut and gashed himself with stones. The wretched demoniac lived naked in the graveyard, wild and seemingly insane. When Jesus encounters the man and asks his name, a demon replies, *"Legion", for many demons had entered him"* (vs. 30). Jesus casts out the legion of demons and the man is set free from his torture. The end of the account finds the man *"clothed and in his right mind"* (vs.35).

Other accounts of demon possession describe the person being thrown into fire or water, heaving with convulsions, or bent over in pain (Mark 917-29, Luke 13:11-13). John MacArthur says, "Scripture presents demon-possessed people as tormented people who suffered wretched indignities" (*Twelve Extraordinary Women* p.174*).

So what can we assume about Mary?

Mary Magdalene would have been a joyless person living a miserable life. She may have been unkempt in her appearance, scarred, or physically maimed in some way. She would have been alone and cast out of home and society. Whatever torment she endured, it was seven-fold and perhaps seven different kinds of torment because she was possessed by seven different demons. Whatever she suffered, however pitiful her past—Jesus set her free. No wonder she loved Him so much.

There has been much speculation about Mary Magdalene. Wild stories have been created about her and Middle Age Gnostics invented legends and lies about her. An apocryphal book was written called *The Gospel of Mary*. It was soundly rejected by the early church fathers as was another false gospel, *The Gospel of Phillip*, which depicted Mary as Peter's rival. In recent years, Dan Brown's book, *The Da Vinci Code*, "discovers" Mary and Jesus are secretly married with children (MacArthur, *Twelve Extraordinary Women*, p. 172). *Jesus Christ Superstar* casts Mary as the lover of Christ, confused about her relationship with Him. Theologians have tried to identify her as the adulterous woman in John 8 or the immoral woman anointing Jesus' feet in Luke 7. But there is no Scriptural evidence that Mary is either of these women or that she was ever immoral—only demon possessed.

And so we must leave it at that. Since the Bible does not give us any details about her past, we must leave her past alone assuming only that it was representative of the misery of demon possession. The great shining truth, however, is that Christ set her free. Oh my! That is enough. **Christ set her free.** It is enough for all of us.

Hope for the past is where some of us need to stop and breathe in the goodness of God. Mary lets us know no life is beyond His grace. No past is too horrific for His forgiveness.

No sin is beyond the reach of His love. No person is without hope.

"Therefore, if any man is in Christ, he is a new creature; the old things passed away; behold, new things have come" (2 Corinthians 5:17). Jesus does not simply clean us up. He makes us new. It is a new birth. A new life. ALL things become new. Salvation is not whitewashing the old person to make us the best person we can be. Salvation is a completely new work, a new creation in Christ. How can that be?

"He [God] made Him [Jesus] who knew no sin to be sin on our behalf that we might become the righteousness of God in Him" (2 Corinthians 5:21). Jesus, the sinless, perfect, Son of God, took our sin upon Himself. He bore it and paid the price for it. But He also gave us His righteousness. He exchanged our sin for His righteousness. In this great exchange, not only has our past been wiped clean but also we have a new standing before God. He does not see us as pitiful, sinful creatures. Instead, He views us as His righteous children. That's why Paul is able to write, *"…forgetting what lies behind, and reaching forward to what lies ahead, I press on…"* (Philippians 3:13-14). Like Paul, you and I can "press on" into the future God has for us. The past has been covered and forgiven. It does not determine the future. We are new creations wearing garments of righteousness.

Romans 8:28 is another layer of hope placed over our past. *"All things work together for good to those who love God and are called according to His purpose."* This promise is not a spiritual Band-Aid, fixing everything to our personal satisfaction. It is, however, a promise that God can use our past, even the consequences of the past, for good. Be careful though. We do not get to define what is good. Only God gets to do that. His definition of good is almost always different from ours simply because His ways are always higher and better. We can, however, trust Him to work out the consequences and the effects of sin for His glory and ultimately our good. God does not erase consequences, but He does redeem them, buying them back and making them into something new. He is able to turn the ashes of the past into robes of beauty.

Jesus dealt with Mary's past by setting her free. She responded with a life of love and service to Him. Christ has the authority and the ability to deal with our pasts as well. Hope is available for each of us. Hope—that sets us free.

Hope for the Present

Being freed from her past, Mary enters a blissful season of life. Luke 8:1-3 gives a glimpse into her new life. Mary is listed with a group of women, counted as faithful followers, who travel with Jesus and His twelve disciples. The women traveled from town to town, listening to Jesus teach, watching Him heal the sick and cast out demons. They also contributed financially to Jesus' ministry. Mary has never known such love and acceptance. She has never lived with such meaningful purpose. She has friends and fellow believers, traveling together, experiencing excitement and hope. It is a sweet season. Surely, Mary never wants it to end.

Mary has come out of terrible darkness to dwell in the light of Christ. Much like the jeweler who displays diamonds against a black velvet background, making the diamond seem more brilliant, Mary's new life is a glimmering contrast to her old one. She is living in the brightest days she has ever known, and she will never take a step backward—only forward into the light of Christ. Perhaps she hopes to travel with Jesus and His entourage for the rest of her days. Perhaps she understands troubles lay ahead but chooses to live joyfully in the radiance of her new, sweet season.

Regardless of Mary's desires, dark days came. Jesus is arrested, tried, and crucified. All four gospels indicate Mary is at the cross—watching her hope die. Other than Jesus' mother, Mary Magdalene must have felt the pain of loss deeper than any other woman. She has been rescued from such darkness. How can she go on? What can she do in the days ahead? Where will she find hope and purpose?

Joseph of Arimathea and Nicodemus claim the body of Jesus after His crucifixion. The Jewish Sabbath is approaching so the men must hurriedly prepare the body for burial. They do not have time to do a thorough job. Laying Jesus' body in a borrowed tomb, Joseph and Nicodemus do the best they can under such duress.

Mary watches it all. She even follows them to the tomb so she will know where to find the body. Mary has plans of her own. When the Sabbath ends, she and two other women will return to the tomb with spices they have purchased. Their intent is to finish the job of anointing Jesus' body (Mark 15:42-16:2).

John 20 gives us further insight into Mary's mindset at the tomb of Jesus. She knows He is dead. Her mind has not yet put together the events of the crucifixion and His message of resurrection. Remember, we have 2000 years of hindsight. Mary is living in the horrible, present-tense moment of death. With a broken heart, Mary weeps. She is not, however, crying softly into her tissue. She is wailing with inconsolable grief.

Christmas came just three months after my late husband's death. I tried hard to make it a normal Christmas for my two sons. It was anything but normal. We blankly opened gifts and then ate our traditional Christmas morning breakfast while staring at each other with empty eyes. Thinking a change of scenery and tradition would be good, the three of us made plans to eat Christmas dinner with friends. When we arrived at their home, my oldest son asked if he could remain in the car for a few minutes before going in. I said yes.

Our friends warmly greeted my youngest son and me. We all hugged, shed a few tears, exchanged gifts, and then suddenly we froze, hearing an unearthly cry just outside the house. It was a sound I had never heard. Deep, primal cries as if an animal were caught in a trap. It could not possibly be a human. But it was.

Alone in the car, my grieving 16-year-old son was wailing. His sorrow, over the loss of his dad, could not be consoled by gifts or friends or a mom desperately trying to make things better. There was no comfort to be had. No joy to be embraced. The cry that pieced our first grieving Christmas was not soft or subtle. It was wild and guttural and barbaric. It was brokenness unleashed. I will never forget the sound.

Can you hear Mary crying at the tomb?

Of all the people surrounding Jesus during His ministry, Mary has the most to lose in His death. Peter and the gang can go back to fishing or family or former jobs. The other women can go home. Even after John and Peter came running to the empty tomb at Mary's bidding, the Bible says they returned to their own homes (John 20:10). But where can Mary go? She has no home. She has no one waiting to welcome her back. She only has a past of darkness. Jesus has been her life. She is distraught to think of anything less.

Mary wants that blissful season back—the season of happiness and endless companionship she has experienced with Jesus and His followers. That season, however, is gone. No amount of longing or crying will ever bring it back.

I remarried a widower with three children just thirteen months after my first husband died. I sold my house in Tennessee and the boys and I relocated to Illinois. Allen had arranged for me and my sons to live with gracious church members while he and I looked for a house suitable for the seven of us. For my two children, moving to a new state, transferring to new schools, and temporarily having no home of our own, only complicated their grief. They began to wither emotionally. I began to panic. It was not a smooth transition.

In the meantime, life rolled along, never taking into account I was a train wreck about to happen. Allen was the pastor and I was his new wife. There were duties to fulfill and events to attend. One event was the annual deacon and wives Christmas party. Even though I had only been in Illinois for a month, I knew as the pastor's wife, I had to be "on" for this event. I had to be polite and kind. I had to look nice and be engaging. I had to pretend there was nowhere else I'd rather be than Southern Illinois with a room full of strangers. My tipping point was getting close.

Since I was still living with church members, Allen came to pick me up for the party. Somewhere between the house and the restaurant, I lost it. I banged my fists on the dashboard of the car and angrily cried, "I want to go home!" I hurled those words over and over at my new husband, pounding my fists to accentuate every word, crying uncontrollably, *"I! Want! To! Go! Home!"*

My practical, logical husband pulled the car to the side of the road and tried to find a solution.

"Jennifer, where is home? If you can tell me where you want to go, I will take you there right now." Allen's words sobered me but did not alter my demand.

"I just want to go home." I downgraded to a whimper.

He continued, "Do you want to go back to Knoxville? Is that home? Remember, you don't have a house there anymore, but if that's where you want to go, I'll take you."

I couldn't respond and my tears only pushed him to ask more questions. "Do you want to go to Chattanooga? Do you want me to take you to your parent's house? Is that home, Jennifer?"

That cold December night, on the side of the road, I realized *home*, for me, was not a location. It was a season. Home was a sweet season when there were only four of us, not seven. Home was a season of security and laugher and maybe a little predictability. It was where my children had normal problems, like schoolwork and girlfriends instead of nightmares and depression. Home was not this grueling season of transition and despair. I wanted to go home. But no matter how earnestly I longed for it, home as I knew it, was gone forever.

Hope, however, does not let go.

Like Mary at the tomb, many of us are not grappling with the past. We are grappling with the difficulty of our present circumstances. We want to go home. We want to go back to a season when the marriage was good, when the child was not a prodigal, when finances were stable, when health was vigorous, when sin had not taken a toll, when life was sweeter. Sadly, those days are gone, and like Mary, we need hope for *this* day and *these* circumstances. Listen, dear one. Jesus is speaking hope.

Mary is alone at the tomb. John and Peter have been there but have returned home. Evidently, the other women have left as well. In her distress, Mary stays. And cries. A man speaks to her and she assumes he is the gardener. She begs for information about the body of Christ. She will be responsible for it if only someone will tell her where it is (John 20:15-16).

"Mary." Jesus speaks her name. She knows it is Him.

In the difficulties of the present, dear reader, Jesus speaks your name. He knows you. He knows everything about you. *"Do not fear. I have redeemed you.* **I have called you by name**, *you are Mine" (Isaiah 43:1).* The relationship He has with you is not simply religion. It is personal. He is not a faraway, fickle God, but a God who is near and knows your name. Matthew 6:25-34 reminds us He is concerned with the smallest details of our lives.

As always, our hope for the present is in Christ. Because of our relationship with Christ, God is working on our behalf, keeping His promises. Biblical hope is not synonymous with restoration of all things lost or a return to life as it used to be. Certainly God can restore or deliver. However, the three young Jewish men in Daniel 3:16-18 remind us, *"Our God is able to deliver us...but even if He does not...."* It is highly probable God will not restore the sweet season you long for. Our hope does not lie in restoration of things as they were. Neither does it lie in deliverance out of difficulties. Hope is in the person of Jesus Christ. Soak in His promises.

He will never leave us or forsake us (Joshua 1:5 & 9, Hebrews 13:5b, Matthew 28:20).

Nothing can snatch us out of His hand (John 10:28).

He will supply all of our needs (Philippians 4:19).

He will strengthen us for every circumstance (Philippians 4:13).

He is working all things together for good (Romans 8:28).

He is accomplishing a good work in us through trials (James 1:2-4).

He has a perfect plan (Jeremiah 29:11).

His grace is sufficient (2 Corinthians 12:9).

All the women we have studied so far do indeed have hope, but they do not necessarily have brighter and better circumstances. Hagar has hope, but God sends her back to slavery for a season. Naomi has hope, but she is still a widow who has also lost two sons. Hannah has hope, but she still must live with Peninnah. Anna has hope, but she remains a widow, advanced in years, living simply in a borrowed room. Martha has hope, but still has to wrestle with that strong personality.

The Samaritan woman has hope, but her past is not magically erased. Not one of these women is miraculously transported to a better moment in time. Likewise, Jesus will not bring back that special season for Mary. Instead He speaks her name, giving her hope for this moment, for this day, and for these circumstances. All of these women live in their present, sometimes difficult circumstances—with hope.

Dear one, do you understand? Because of our hope in Christ, our souls can be anchored even when the marriage is tough, even when the child is still a prodigal, even when finances are tight, even when health is precarious, even when consequences of sin remain. The anchor of hope is not dependent on the absence of difficulty. The anchor holds, precious believer, in the middle of the difficulty!

Hope for the Future

Hope is always forward looking, anticipating the goodness of God's promises in Christ. When Jesus has Mary's attention, He immediately gives her a new purpose. He gives her hope for the days ahead as He speaks two commands to her. "*Let go*" and "*go tell*" will define her future (John 20:17-18).

Jesus tells Mary to stop clinging to Him, to *let go*. After all, she can hardly believe her eyes. It is really Him! Now she is not sobbing with grief but with relief and joy, hanging onto her Savoir lest He leave her again. As a woman, maybe she is a hugger— hugging His feet, hugging His neck. Hugging, stepping back to make sure it is all real, then hugging again.

While there may be theological reasons for Jesus' request to *let go,* there may be a more practical reason as well. Jesus is letting Mary know things are not as they used to be. She has to let go of her expectation of life returning to "normal". She has to understand the joy of the moment is not the ultimate goal. She cannot keep Jesus in her sight as before. She will have to trust Him on a new and higher level. Letting go will be hard for Mary, but she must *let go* in order to fulfill the second command, *go tell.*

Certainly, the Lord is not asking Mary or us to let go of our relationship with Him. He is, however, assuring us that while He never lets go of us, we sometimes must release our preconceived ideas about the future. We must let go of the plans we have formulated for ourselves and prepare to embrace the plans He has for our future. Often I have heard well-meaning Christians tell people to "dream big." The fallacy of that mindset is we often miss the things God has designed for us. We are so intent on hanging on to our plans and dreams we never see or embrace the plans of God.

Surrender is the key here. Trusting God's character enough to know He is not going to dash our plans, but rather He will broaden and enrich our future in ways we never imagined. He knows the plans He has for us (Jeremiah 29:11), so we must trust Him enough to let go of our own plans. *Letting go* may be difficult but it carries a sense of anticipation as well. As we let go, we begin to live in the hope of God's plan and God's future for our lives.

Jesus gives Mary a new purpose. No longer will she have the sweet days of following Jesus in His earthly ministry, but she will have the blessed responsibility of telling others about Him. Jesus gives Mary the job of returning to the disciples, telling them what she has seen and heard. Jesus is alive! She has experienced it, touched Him, spoken with Him. She will be the first eye witness to the good news of His resurrection.

While it may seem small to us, the command to "*go tell*" was monumental for a woman of that day. Women were not viewed as a reliable source of information. In fact, a woman was not allowed to testify in Jewish court because her words were not considered trustworthy. But Jesus chooses to entrust the good news of His resurrection to a woman with a past. A woman with seemingly no future. A woman whose life would never be "normal" again.

Jesus could have given the assignment to Peter or John. Those men were just there at the tomb. Jesus knew they had been there. He was probably watching the entire scene. Jesus could have given the job of "*go tell*" to someone deemed more reliable and less broken. But He doesn't. He gives the job to Mary Magdalene.

There is great hope for you and me in Jesus' words to Mary. While society chooses the best and brightest among us, Jesus chooses the wounded and broken. Jesus chooses the least likely and by grace gives them a new identity and a new purpose. Scripture is filled with examples.

Shepherds were the lowest rung of ancient Jewish society, considered ceremonially unclean because of their work with animals. Yet God chose the unfit shepherds to herald the good news of the Savior's birth (Luke 2:8-20). Likewise, the Geresene demoniac was an outcast, ruined man. Yet Jesus delivered him and gave him the command to *go home and tell* all that Christ had done (Luke 8:39). Wouldn't someone else have been a better mouthpiece of good news? Remember the Samaritan woman? The woman who had serious relationship issues? Jesus offered her hope and cleansing. In turn, she became the voice of hope for her entire region.

In ancient Japan, if a piece of pottery were cracked or broken, the potter repaired the broken piece with gold. The value of the gold transformed the broken object into an object of beauty. The broken place was no longer a detriment. Instead, it became a unique piece of the object's history.

Similarly, when broken, wounded, insignificant, or cast-aside people encounter Christ, He transforms their lives and gives them hope. They become the most effective bearers of light and witnesses of the good news of Christ. Out of brokenness, beauty is born.

The Apostle Paul put it this way:

"Consider your calling, brethren, that there were not many wise according to the flesh, not many mighty, not many noble; but God has chosen the foolish things of the world to shame the wise, and God has chosen the weak things of the world to shame the things which are strong, and the base things of the world and the despised, God has chosen, the things that are not, that He might nullify the things that are, that no man should boast before God" (1 Corinthians 1:26-28).

When explaining this passage of Scripture, my college pastor often said, "God uses more *nobodies* than *somebodies*. But He will make a *somebody* out of a *nobody*." That is great news for people like Mary and people like us—people who have brokenness in their past and difficulties in their present. Christ gives hope for tomorrow. He gives purpose for the next season of life. He is the God of hope and with that hope, He gives joy and peace (Romans 15:13).

Personally, my present and my future look vastly different than what I envisioned for myself. There has been no return to the sweet season of the past. Yet in His grace, God has provided a new season of hope.

Shortly after my first husband died, an older woman sent me a kind note which included a passage of Scripture. At the time, I could not understand how the truth of these verses could apply to me. Now, however, I see them through the eyes of hope as God is speaking to His people. The verses sent to me by that dear lady are among my favorite passages of Scripture.

"Do not call to mind the former things, or ponder things of the past. Behold, I will do something new, now it will spring forth; will you not be aware of it? I will even make a roadway in the wilderness, rivers in the desert" (Isaiah 43:18-19).

For the rest of her days, Mary will speak about the past, present, and future framed in hope. She will tell of the resurrected Christ and the hope He gives in each season of life. Certainly, the Lord has created a river in the desert of her life. Her soul is anchored in the daily, living hope of Jesus Christ.

Dear reader, this hope is for you as well. Hope to cover your past. Hope in the difficulties of the present. Hope for the future. Like Mary Magdalene, your hope is in Christ. He is your hope in every season of life.

Discussion Questions

Read Luke 8:1-3, John 20:1-18

1. The Lord cares about every season and every detail of our lives. Read Matthew 6:25-34. How do these verses address the season of life you are in right now?

2. Read Philippians 3:13-14 and Romans 8:28. Does God expect us to forget our past? The Lord often uses someone else's past to encourage us or help us. Can you think of a time when someone else's story of redemption and forgiveness has helped you?

3. Read Jeremiah 29:11. What is the difference between "dreaming big" and trusting God with your future?

4. Read Isaiah 43:1. God calls us by name! What does this truth mean to you?

5. How is the Lord working today—in this season of your life?

Thoughts and Suggestions for Facilitators of Small Group Bible Studies

This book can easily be adapted for an eight week small group Bible study. For participants, there are no homework assignments other than reading the next chapter.

After the foundation is laid in Chapter One, each lesson stands alone, allowing for flexibility in attendance. Unforeseen circumstances sometimes prevent busy women from attending every week of Bible study. This study is designed to allow participants to easily return after an absence. Important themes and Scripture passages are repeated in several chapters. Even if a participant misses a week, similar themes will recur throughout the study.

Encourage each participant to stay current on reading, even if she cannot attend the scheduled meeting.

As a leader, mark each chapter with your own thoughts and questions as you read and prepare for the weekly gathering. Read the discussion questions at the end of each chapter ahead of time. Bring your own knowledge of Scripture to the discussion. Keep in mind, opinions are valuable but Scripture is the ultimate authority. Encourage discussion that always points participants to Christ and His Word.

Some chapters tackle difficult issues. Be sensitive. Not everyone is willing to share their personal story.

Pray for one another. As your small group becomes comfortable with each other, hopefully they will become more open as well. Encourage group members to pray for each other throughout the week.

Blessings, dear woman, as you facilitate a small group. I have prayed for you in advance!

Acknowledgements

I am thankful to the Lord for every person who has encouraged me in this endeavor. If not for the team around me, writing could easily become a lonely exercise in overthinking.

Thank you to a wonderful group of women who each have a clear eye for details and a teacher's heart. **Trina Aker, Karen Murphree, Marcia Bickmore, and Susan McKenzie** have graciously corrected errors, made suggestions, helped formulate discussion questions, and covered the entire process with prayer and grace. I am humbled by your skill, your kindness, and your friendship.

Thank you to every person who has allowed me to tell their story. Even though some names and details have been altered for the sake of privacy, each person lovingly gave their permission and their blessing so that others might be helped. I pray each of your stories continue to bear good fruit as you allow the Lord to use you.

Thank you to my husband Allen. When I became weary of writing and was tempted to quit, you encouraged me to press on. I am immensely thankful for your tenacity and leadership, as well as your patience during the process of completing *Women of Hope*. You are a gift from the Lord, an unexpected blessing in an unexpected season of life. I love you.

Thank you to Tim Passmore and Outcome Publishing for graciously working with me over the past four years. You are meeting a great need in the publishing world and for me personally.

Thank you to every person who has partnered with me through *Word of Joy*. You have contributed to this endeavor in countless ways. You have invested in my life and I am often overwhelmed by the goodness of God demonstrated through you.